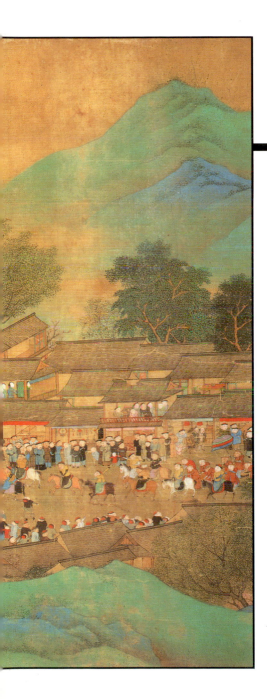

FENG SHUI

HANDBOOK

*How to Create a Healthier Living
and Working Environment*

MASTER LAM KAM CHUEN

An Owl Book
Henry Holt and Company
New York

A Henry Holt Reference Book
Henry Holt and Company, Inc.
Publishers since 1866
115 West 18th Street
New York, New York 10011

First published in the United States in 1996
by Henry Holt and Company, Inc.
Published in Canada by Fitzhenry & Whiteside Ltd.,
195 Allstate Parkway, Markham, Ontario L3R 4T8.
Originally published in the United Kingdom in 1996
by Gaia Books Ltd.

Library of Congress Cataloging-in-Publication Data
Chuen, Lam Kam.
   Feng Shui handbook: how to create a healthier living and
working environment / Master Lam Kam Chuen.
     p. cm. – (A Henry Holt reference book)
     Includes bibliographical references and index.
   1. Feng-shui.   I. Title.   II. Series.
BF1779.F4C4855 1996   95-17234
                                         CIP
133.3'33–dc20

ISBN 0-8050-4215-6

Henry Holt books are available for special promotions and
premiums. For details contact: Director, Special Markets.

First American Edition – 1996

Printed in Hong Kong through Bookbuilders Ltd
All first editions are printed on acid-free paper. ∞

10 9 8 7

FRONTISPIECE *The Emperor Kang Shi's tour of Kiang-Han by Chaio Ping Chen (1661–1722)*

Contents

Introduction

You walk into a room and your host tells you to make yourself at home. What do you do and where do you sit?

You are looking for a new house and after looking at dozens of places you walk into one that immediately feels right.

You have lived in the same place for years and one day you suddenly decide that it needs to be completely redecorated.

You are told your office is moving. You visit the new site and the next thing you do is start looking for a new job.

This natural sensitivity is part of the priceless heritage of being human. It is an instinct that can be developed and trained. Learning how to do that is the subject of this book.

It is a book about places and people, and the way the energies of both interact. It is based on humanity's longest, unbroken tradition of research into the innermost secrets of nature. Yet it is designed to help people living in today's world. You don't have to be an architect to use this book. You don't have to be an interior designer. You don't have to be Chinese or speak Chinese. All you have to do is begin with your own living situation, your own feelings, and your own room.

Living rooms
Rooms live. They are fields of energy. Your feelings about rooms and buildings are profound. Your innate sense tells you that more is involved than simply interior décor. Look at the room pictured on the facing page. If you walk into that room, do you know automatically where you want to sit, or do you hesitate? Do you find the room welcoming or disturbing? Everyone's reactions will vary, but those reactions themselves are determined by powerful forces in our personalities.

Our feelings about the room depend in part on the assumptions we make about what will happen while we are in it. Is it a room in which we expect to work, to eat, to meet people, or to sleep? Is it a room in which we intend to spend many hours of our lives, or one through which we are just passing? We react differently to these different uses of the room. The role its energy will play in our lives deeply influences our feelings about the colors, the bright spotlights, the metallic furniture, and the two open doorways.

Those feelings are more than passing emotional states. They are often health warnings. They tell us that if we sit without proper support at our backs, we may be approached without warning from the rear. They tell us that our sleep may be disturbed if there is an open window over our bed. In every moment of our lives we pick up these messages. They tell us that we are profoundly interconnected with our environments and that the energies that surround us shape our lives and our futures.

A used book
This book is meant to be used. It is not a theoretical treatise but a beginner's manual. It has been carefully designed to introduce you to certain fundamental concepts and principles first. These are set out in Part One. This foundation is important since, without it, the practical advice that follows in Part Two may be difficult to appreciate. You are, therefore, strongly advised to read this book from the beginning and not to dip into it at random. When you get to Part Two, you will find numerous cross-references, which show how the practical advice flows from the theory. Bear in mind, at all times, that the information in this book is suitable for a beginner's introduction to the subject; the serious study of Feng Shui can literally take decades.

At various points throughout the book you will find photo essays that give an interpretation of famous buildings around the world. These include Buckingham Palace, the US Capitol, the United

Nations, and the Taj Mahal. Each building is assessed using Feng Shui principles, revealing key aspects of its strengths or weaknesses, and the effect it has on people associated with it.

Culture crossing

The journey from one culture to another is a difficult crossing. It is also profoundly illuminating because it teaches us as much about ourselves and our assumptions as it does about others.

For many, the first encounter with Feng Shui (pronounced "Fung Shoy") can be compared to discovering a new language. It can throw up the same resistances we have when confronted for the first time with a new alphabet, new phonetics, and new structures of thought. As we penetrate it, we risk the shock of finding concepts expressed by the new language that have not been developed in our own and for which no translation seems possible.

In some respects, Feng Shui is as unique to China as its language. It is an art at the very pinnacle of the social, cultural, and scientific achievements of Chinese civilization. Yet at the same time, it deals with the common experience of all humanity as we learn how best to live on this earth – our common home in space. It is an analytical system developed, not by one person, but by a centuries-old cumulative tradition based on meticulous observation and experimentation. Its roots lie in the soil of China, but its very name – simply "Wind and Water" – speaks to the age-old search for our home in Nature.

To some, Feng Shui is pure superstition, just as fearing a black cat that crosses your path is. The Feng Shui master's answer to this is simple. Wind and Water are present whether you believe in them or not, just as oxygen and hydrogen atoms are. We don't know the secrets of wheat, fire, and electricity, yet we make and eat bread; don't let your ignorance of Feng Shui deprive you of its benefits!

This book is an attempt to bring those benefits to the Western world. It takes the deep wisdom of the Chinese classics and distills from their complexity essential advice that can be applied in the contemporary world. At the same time, it tries to avoid some of the pitfalls of the D-I-Y approach to this art. At the heart of Feng Shui lies a profound sensitivity to the uniqueness of all things and all moments, and an awareness of the fact that they are constantly changing. Therefore there can be no firm, final answers and no automatic, enduring solutions. Every person, every family, every home, every office, every day, and every place is different – there are some common principles, but no rules.

Failure to appreciate this fundamental world view has led to misunderstandings about Feng Shui and to assumptions that off-the-rack solutions are on offer. Even worse are the misinformed practices that exist. For example, putting goldfish in bowls to attract negative energy in the belief that if the fish die, it is a sign that we have been spared bad luck.

Often people's first contact with Feng Shui comes when they enter the unique cultural mix of Hong Kong. If you travel there on business you may well be told by other expatriates that people who believe in Feng Shui are crazy, but that at the same time if you don't take Feng Shui advice you are stupid! This book may help you make up your mind.

Looking different

Many things will look different to you after reading this book. You may find parts of it irritating. Some of it may challenge the way you see the world around you and some of it may trouble you. For example, if you have just installed a fish pond or swimming pool in your back garden, you probably won't like the advice about water throughout this book. If you live in a small open-plan apartment, you may be upset if you have little or no space in which to make changes. Some people may also be upset because the wisdom in this book directly contradicts some very widespread practices that prevail in construction and design, both in the home and the workplace.

You may be surprised by the strength of your feelings as you work through the book and begin to look at your home, your neighbourhood, and your workplace through new eyes. Reactions range from disbelief and dismissiveness through to anger and guilt. If you choose not to accept the advice in these pages, you are perfectly entitled to make that decision. You may even be lucky, because you will not then be troubled by any of the discrepancies between the information you find here and the way you actually live.

But if you want to improve your quality of life, you may be unsettled by this book. You may start looking at everything around you and deciding it is wrong. Perhaps you can see no way in which to make the necessary changes, or simply can't afford to make them. So you feel guilty about that. You can even go to the extreme of thinking that you have been a poor parent because you have allowed your children to sleep for years under a beam in the roof!

Such reactions are very real and deeply human. But they are based on a misunderstanding. The advice in this book is not dogmatic. There are no absolute rules in this system and there is no concept of perfection. Just as people live long lives in circumstances that may, in theory, be very unhealthy, so we continue to live fully in all sorts of environments. The best approach to follow is this: if you see something that you want to change and can do it, then go ahead; if, for any reason, you can't make the change, then put it out of your mind. If you want to return to the idea later, when it is more appropriate, fine, but don't allow this book to become a perpetual source of anxiety.

The experimental approach

Suppose you want to apply the principles in this book to your life in a serious way. You want to consult a Feng Shui expert, but you have no way of finding one. How can you use this book? The best approach is to be truly experimental. This requires the scientific virtues of keen observation, patience, and an open mind. Say you want to reorganize your bedroom. Then begin by making one change in line with the advice in this book, such as changing the position of the light beside your bed or switching the position of the bed and table in your room. Be alert to what happens to you over the ensuing three weeks.

At the end of the three weeks ask yourself if anything unfortunate happened to you that was out of the ordinary. Don't worry about where it happened or how or why, just recollect any accidents or unusually difficult moments. If you did have some unusual bad luck of any kind, then go back to the original arrangement in the room and try to make another change. Then follow the same self-diagnostic process over a three-week period.

This slow, methodical approach has certain advantages. It will heighten your powers of observation and you will start to adjust your living arrangements in accordance with your real circumstances. You will be engaged in a process far more authentic than simply rushing around with a book in one hand and a compass in the other. But this personal experimentation is no substitute for the professional advice of an authentic Feng Shui practitioner, especially since an expert can advise you on the basis of calculations involving time and the Chinese calendar. It is rather like buying some commercially available medication for a sore throat – if it works, fine; but if the condition persists, you need to see a doctor!

A final word of advice. Simply by virtue of being alive, we have all developed certain habits and we feel very comfortable with them. They are our way of coping with the experience of living. If you encounter some advice in this book that runs completely counter to the way you live – and you are satisfied that the way you live is well suited to you – then follow your own instincts. If life is going well for you as things are, it could be a mistake to change them. Listen to your own experience.

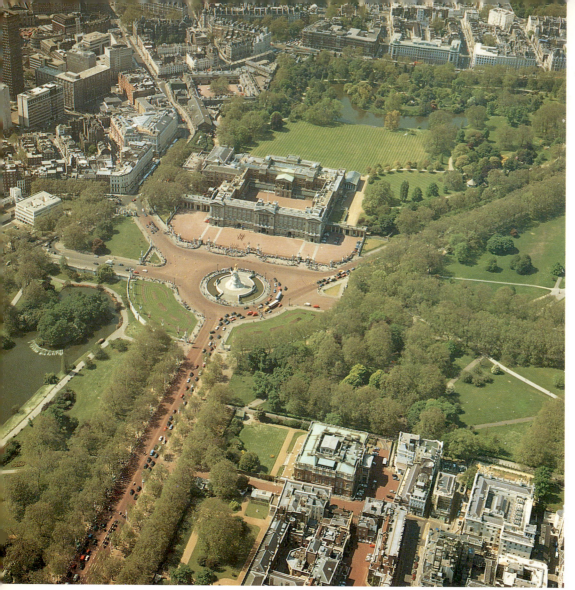

Grand design

Seen from above, the extravagant layout of Buckingham Palace (above) is revealed with its outer lines of protection. To the rear, the stately gardens offer a calm expanse undisturbed by pathways and surrounded by distant trees. The long line of approach up The Mall could be a line of energy streaming in like an attacking force, straight toward the forecourt. The Queen Victoria memorial is brilliantly positioned to deflect oncoming forces.

Safe haven

The Forbidden City (above), the seat of Chinese Emperors in Beijing, was laid out under the supervision of the imperial masters of Feng Shui. Here, just inside the outermost walls, is the artificially created river, the "Water" of Feng Shui, which curves lazily across this outer courtyard, protecting the approach to the

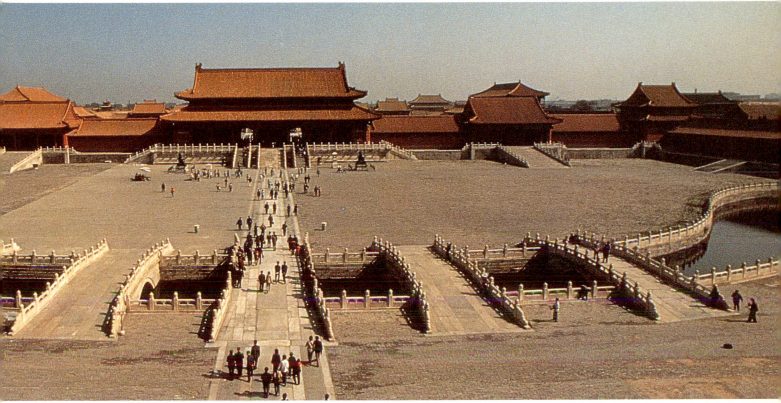

central palaces. The fact
that there are five bridges
has numerological significance, reflecting the figure
at the center of the Chinese
number box (see pp. 26-7)
and the central power of
the ruler. Only the
Emperor's party proceeded
up the central bridge and
avenue of the City; the
bridges on either side were
for the other officials of the
court and their retinue.

Lonely tower
The United Nations skyscraper (left) rises
in solitude on the banks of New York's
East River. It is a perfect example of one of
the fundamental principles in Feng Shui:
buildings are like living beings and cannot
thrive in isolation. The lonely tower soars
skyward, a figure of majesty that lacks support – it is like a king without generals or
soldiers, a building that needs support but
cannot get it. Its very location is insecure:
water to the rear is always avoided in Feng
Shui, and constantly pointing a slender finger of disturbance is the knife-like line of
Roosevelt Island.

11

Mountain view, a watercolor
from the Ming period.

PART ONE

The fundamental forces

Ancient history, eternal principle

The Chinese art of arranging one's life in accordance with the forces of the universe stretches back over at least 7000 years and probably far further. It is a profoundly creative and intuitive art. But it is also a science, with diagnostic equipment, mathematical formulas, and specialized terminology.

The art is rooted in an extraordinary sensitivity to nature. This affinity with the natural world is reflected in the two Chinese ideograms that make up its name: Feng Shui. The literal meaning of the words Feng Shui, pronounced "Fung Shoy", is Wind and Water.

The natural universe

Wind and Water are two of the most fundamental forms of life's energy. We know from our own experience how essential both are to us. Without air we die within seconds. While we can live for weeks without food, without water we soon perish. In Feng Shui, the ideograms Wind and Water also have a broader meaning because separately and together they symbolize manifestations of the movement of energy. Once we begin to see our world in this way, we can look at our environments and their characteristics in a completely different light.

As contemplation and exploration of the natural universe evolved in China, Feng Shui practitioners made increasingly subtle discoveries, of both a philosophical and practical nature. They were able to identify the ways in which the natural energy around them behaved and how it affected them. This information could then be used to establish favourable locations for human habitation and the auspicious confluence of forces for healthy and harmonious living.

By the time Feng Shui emerged as a fully fledged system, the eternal "art of finding one's place", it brought together the eight strands of thought and practice shown on the facing page. At the center of the matrix, stood the constant factor of the

individual human being, bringing the total number of elements involved to nine: the nine aspects of Feng Shui. Each element is explained in the pages that follow.

WIND

WATER

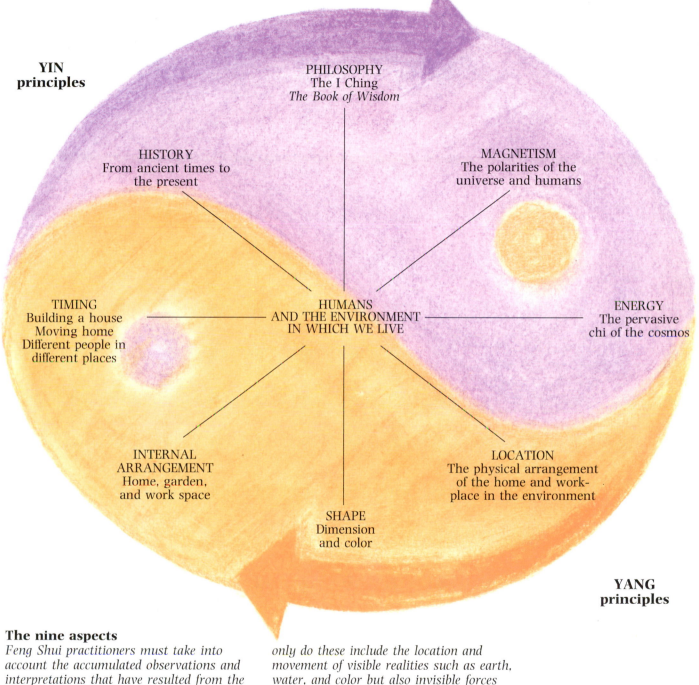

YIN principles

PHILOSOPHY
The I Ching
The Book of Wisdom

MAGNETISM
The polarities of the
universe and humans

HISTORY
From ancient times to
the present

TIMING
Building a house
Moving home
Different people in
different places

HUMANS
AND THE ENVIRONMENT
IN WHICH WE LIVE

ENERGY
The pervasive
chi of the cosmos

INTERNAL
ARRANGEMENT
Home, garden,
and work space

LOCATION
The physical arrangement
of the home and work-
place in the environment

SHAPE
Dimension
and color

YANG principles

The nine aspects

Feng Shui practitioners must take into account the accumulated observations and interpretations that have resulted from the practice of their art over the centuries. Not only do these include the location and movement of visible realities such as earth, water, and color but also invisible forces like magnetism, time, and change.

The beginning of all things

"Knowing the ancient beginning is the essence of the Way", wrote the Chinese sage Lao Tse in the Tao Teh Ching. His perception of the origin of all that exists, poetically referred to as the "ten thousand things", was based on a centuries-old tradition of the meticulous contemplation of the natural world.

Early Western scientific observation focused primarily on the behaviour of material objects. But the Chinese tradition became acutely aware of the more intangible background of energetic influences and life forces that create the objects and beings around us. As a consequence, the Chinese contemplated the fathomless and indeterminate space out of which all phenomena emerge and became aware of the invisible, limitless potential of the universe. Difficult to express in everyday mundane language, this concept has often been mistranslated and mis-interpreted by the use of seemingly negative terms such as "Void" or "Nothingness" – implying a kind of dark, uninhabited vacuum that evokes the pathology of depression.

In reality, the meaning is exactly the opposite. The beginning of everything is nothing. Out of the mystery of nothing the miracle of everything emerges. Not "nothing" in the sense of non-existence, but in the same sense as when we look up into a cloudless sky at dawn and watch patient-ly, we see clouds apparently materializing out of what was a clear, empty sky. The Chinese expressed this potential of energy by drawing a perfect circle. As a symbol, it succeeds where words fail – expressing at a stroke both fullness and empti-ness, endless motion and complete tranquillity. The Chinese refer to it as "Wu Chi", which conveys the meaning of "primal energy".

The Chinese understood the circle to be a womb or an unfertilized egg. Both are full of life, ready to give birth, able to give material expression to the intense vitality of growth. The moment a sperm enters the egg, transformation occurs. Within the circle, a tiny dot appears and changes the energetic pattern. What was dormant is now fertilized. What

The birth of Yin and Yang
Rooted in accurate analysis of the natural world, the Chinese perceived the movements of universal energy in the unfolding of life on the earth. The circle, a fertilized egg, is transformed by a single sperm, represented by the dot.

The Wu Chi
All primal energy is expressed by and contained within the circle that is full and empty at the same time. "Mysteriously formed before heaven and earth... it is the mother of the ten thousand things." Tao Teh Ching

was previously undifferentiated has now begun to acquire characteristics. The single entity is now divided. The Chinese call this the birth of Yin and Yang – the emergence of the two fundamental, interactive forces of the universe.

At this very earliest moment of transformation, nothing moves. Two different potentials emerge, rather like creating a magnetic field. Two poles now exist. The force fields of their polarized

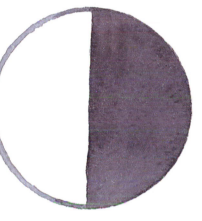

The emerging forces
Yin and Yang are the Way of heaven and earth, the fundamental principle of the myriad things, the father and mother of change and transformation. The twin forces of Yin and Yang act upon each other. Movement is initiated.

energies begin to grow so that the entire space of the original circle becomes a playground for the growing forces of Yin and Yang. The ancient depiction of this stage is a circle divided in half, one side light, one side dark.

The forces are so finely balanced and so interdependent that their movement resembles two fish gliding together in water. This extraordinary motif is as elegant a description of the fundamental character of the known universe as the most subtle algebraic formula. The outer circle continues to represent the totality of all existence, together with its undifferentiated potential. The interpenetrating forces of Yin and Yang are in balanced motion. Where Yin is least, Yang is greatest. Where Yang declines, Yin grows. In the centre of both segments,

there is a small circle – a seed of Yin within the abundance of Yang, the origin of Yang within the fullness of Yin. In this way, endlessly, Yin and Yang give birth to each other.

The Yin/Yang model deserves and rewards prolonged contemplation. Everything that follows in this book is rooted in this theoretical model of the universe. Most significant of all is a perception, inherent in the Yin/Yang theory, which is very different to much conventional thinking. Many of our assumptions about the world around us tend to be based on the idea of the existence of inert matter on the one hand (rocks or hammers) and forms of energy on the other (lightning or thought). We now know that this is an illusion. Contemporary physics – and the explosion of the atom and hydrogen bombs – have shown that matter and energy are fundamentally one and the same. Feng Shui is based on the same realization. The Feng Shui world looks far more like our own seen under a powerful microscope – a world in which the apparently solid dissolves into a dance of energy, a world whose essential characteristics are constantly transformed from one manifestation into another, in which all energetic patterns affect each other.

The Tai Chi
All things and events grow and develop unceasingly, expressing the perpetual exchange of Yin and Yang.

Light and shadow

Yin and Yang can be seen in everything around us. The instant light falls upon an object, there is both illumination and shadow. The Chinese characters for Yin and Yang depict the effect of sunlight on a hill. One side is bathed in light, the other falls in shadow. Both characters have several components.

Yin is composed of a hill, a cloud in the sky, and people gathered together under a single roof.

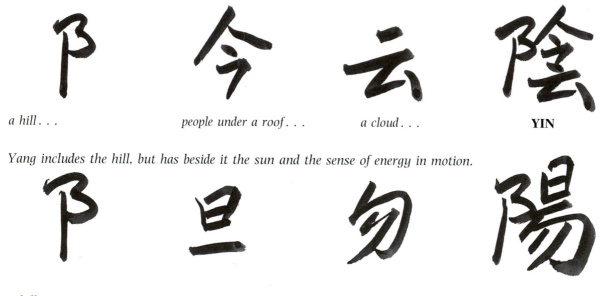

a hill...   people under a roof...   a cloud...   **YIN**

Yang includes the hill, but has beside it the sun and the sense of energy in motion.

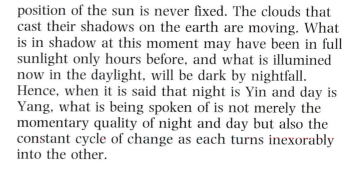

a hill...   sun above the horizon...   rays of light, moving energy...   **YANG**

Yin expresses the subtle feeling we have when we see the side of the hill in shadow. The mood of Yang is that of a hillside in bright sunlight. Arising from this metaphor, Yin is commonly thought of as darkness and shade, Yang as brightness and light.

Chinese characters convey far more than simple static states. They are evocative, like poetry. Because the play of sunlight on a hillside displays a changeable, transitory quality we can experience at first hand the interaction of Yin and Yang. The position of the sun is never fixed. The clouds that cast their shadows on the earth are moving. What is in shadow at this moment may have been in full sunlight only hours before, and what is illumined now in the daylight, will be dark by nightfall. Hence, when it is said that night is Yin and day is Yang, what is being spoken of is not merely the momentary quality of night and day but also the constant cycle of change as each turns inexorably into the other.

At any moment, the elusive quality of Yin or Yang can be discerned in everything that we experience. Wherever we see the energetic quality of someone or something being receptive, there is Yin – the power of nurturing and giving birth. The power of directive, forceful activity, on the other hand, is Yang. As the accompanying chart shows, these powers become evident in many ways.

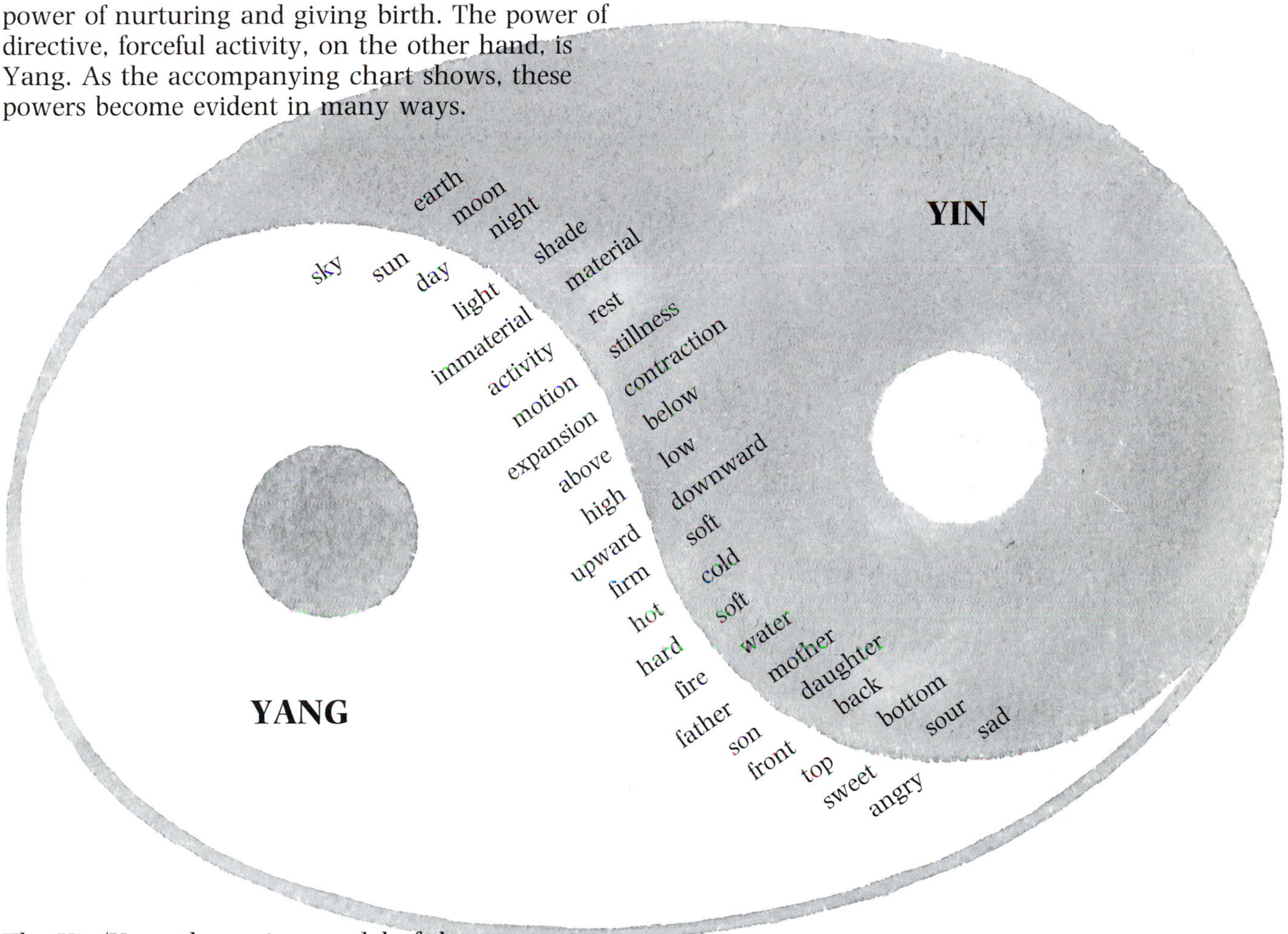

YIN

YANG

earth
moon
night
shade
material
sky
sun
day
light
rest
stillness
inmaterial
contraction
activity
below
motion
low
expansion
downward
above
high
soft
upward
cold
firm
soft
hot
water
hard
mother
daughter
fire
back
bottom
father
son
sour
sad
front
top
sweet
angry

The Yin/Yang theory is a model of the constant process of change. In this particular sense, Yin and Yang merely mark two points – at any one moment – in the transformation of energy. Nothing is fundamentally Yin or Yang in and of itself. Nothing exists in separation from the rest of the universe. Even if we could isolate anything, we couldn't prevent it from changing.

La Défense, Paris

The interaction of Yin and Yang is all pervasive. In this cityscape the land, which is solid, is Yin; the motion in the sky overhead is Yang. The curved lines of the buildings are more Yin in relation to the straight, vertical and horizontal lines, which are more Yang. The concrete pavement and the buildings are stable and still, and hence Yin in relation to the vitality and movement of the passing human beings, who are Yang. But the same buildings, in relation to their shadows, are Yang because these are solid structures, whereas the emptiness of the shadows is Yin. The shadows, being dark, are Yin as opposed to the Yang of the light. But these same shadows are constantly in motion so that areas which are now in shade will soon be in sunlight; what was once Yin will have become Yang.

Clew Bay, Ireland

You can apply Yin and Yang theory to this land-scape. The daylight is Yang in relationship to the inevitable arrival of night-fall, and the sun itself is Yang in relation to the earth. The clouds are soft, cool, and moist. Therefore they are Yin in relation to the sun. But the clouds, in relation to the shadows that they cast, are far brighter and therefore Yang in relation to the shade below them. The mountains, in relation to the lowlands, are Yang. But, in relation to the lake, they are Yin – since the mountains are still and the water in the lake is flowing. At the same time, the fluid, yielding quality of the water is Yin in relation to the upward-rising and solid energy of the moun-tain. The walls of the hous-es in shadow are Yin in relation to the sides in the light. But this relationship is not something that will endure: it too will change with the passing of time.

The patterns of change

Yin and Yang give birth to the countless patterns of existence. Universal designs emerge out of the bewildering profusion of beings and events. The transformations of energy can be systematically charted. To do this is a vast enterprise, accomplished by Chinese scholars thousands of years ago in a remarkable work of wisdom, the I Ching, best known as *The Book of Changes*. This compendium of meticulous observations offers a complex and comprehensive manual for understanding the constant flux that is continually creating and changing the world in which we live.

At the heart of *The Book of Changes* lies the theory of Yin and Yang. Its 64 chapters – and the many commentaries by distinguished Chinese philosophers down through the ages – carefully trace the way in which the interaction of Yin and Yang produce all the constantly changing phenomena we experience.

Now available in several translations, *The Book of Changes* is one of the most prodigious works ever undertaken by the human mind and has exercised a powerful influence not only over centuries of Chinese culture, but on great minds down the ages the world over.

Regular consultation of *The Book of Changes* as a source of divination has led to intense speculation about its nature and value. In China alone, several hundred commentaries have been written to interpret the meaning of its structure and cryptic statements. But the importance of the work lies not merely in its value as a tool of prediction but in its startling insights into the inner mechanisms of change. "Like a part of nature," wrote the psychologist Carl Jung, "it waits until it is discovered".

The characteristics of change – and their resulting patterns – are analyzed in *The Book of Changes* using a deceptively simple set of eight trigrams. Each trigram consists of three lines. Each line, in turn, is either broken or unbroken. The broken line represents the force of Yin, the female principle, and the unbroken line symbolizes the force of Yang, the male principle.

The eight trigrams
Out of Wu Chi (the perfect circle representing both totality and emptiness) are born Yin and Yang. When Yin (female) and Yang (male) interact, they produce two sons and two daughters. Each of the sons and daughters, in turn, produce a further son and daughter, thus creating the eight fundamental trigrams.

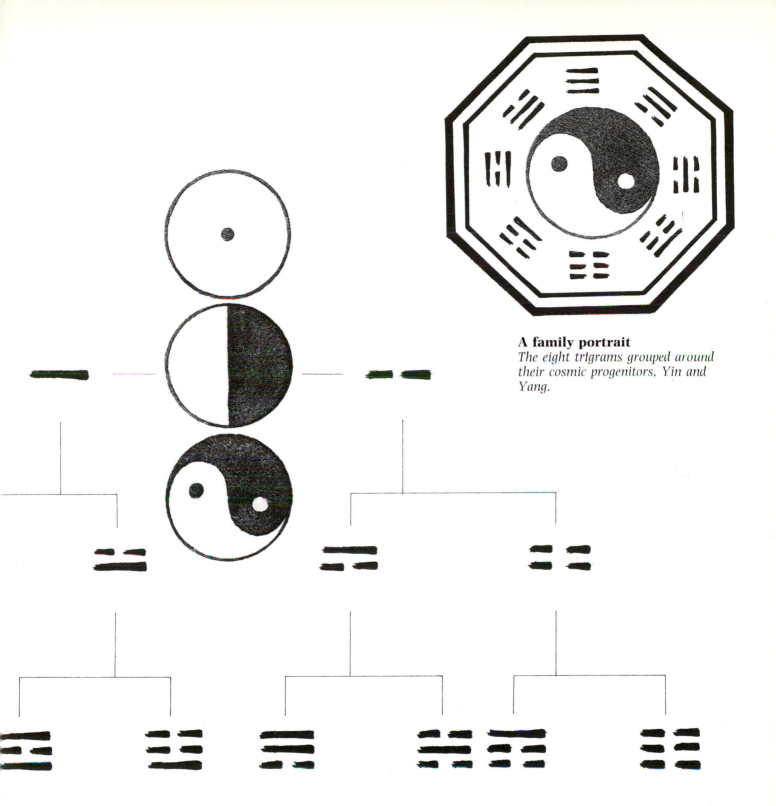

A family portrait
The eight trigrams grouped around their cosmic progenitors, Yin and Yang.

23

The ten thousand things

Yin and Yang constantly change into each other. Their combinations are therefore in constant flux. As we have seen, the possible combinations grow as they combine: first two, then four, then eight. The permutations of the eight produce 64 pairs of trigrams – the 64 hexagrams of the I Ching. Out of their interaction comes the multiplicity of the "ten thousand things".

To interpret the 64 hexagrams you must understand the original significance of the eight trigrams. They are said to have been divined by Fu Hsi, a king who may have lived around 3000 BCE. The trinities of Yin and Yang lines that make up the eight trigrams represent all the fundamental conditions on earth and in the cosmos.

The family of lines

Traditionally, the eight trigrams were thought of as a family that represented the primary configuration of energetic forces in every aspect of life. The sequence below is the original order into which they were first organized.

FATHER The Chinese name is Ch'ien, meaning Heaven. The three solid strokes indicate maximum Yang power, evoking a feeling of the great creative power and strength throughout nature. This is the force of inspiration, of leadership, of will power and determination.

YOUNGEST DAUGHTER The Chinese name is Tui – the Lake. The softer broken Yin line rests on the support of two Yang lines, as a new child is supported by the rest of the family. The feeling here is very fresh, the quality of being alert and attractive. This is also the power of communication, pleasure, and open-heartedness.

MIDDLE DAUGHTER The Chinese name is Li – Fire. Two Yang lines are pushed apart by the power of a single Yin line in the middle. The energy here is explosive, pushing two forces apart from within. There is a sense of the power of illumination, of clarity and intelligence.

ELDEST SON The Chinese name is Chen – Thunder. The force of a single Yang line on the bottom is emerging upward through the two Yin lines above it. But also, like the eldest son in a traditional family, the Yang power gives support to those who depend upon it. The concept of Thunder conveys the power and speed of a spark born of the forces of Yin and Yang – the irresistible release of stored energy.

ELDEST DAUGHTER The Chinese name is Sun – the Wind. The penetrating energy of a single Yin line presses upward against two solid Yang lines. The energy is seemingly gentle and invisible, yet it is persistent, patient, and hard-working. Just as you might fan others on a hot day, you work quietly yourself and the breeze is felt by others.

MIDDLE SON The Chinese name is Hum (K'an) – Water. The outside lines of this trigram are two soft Yin lines. Within them is a strong Yang line. This expresses the mysterious power of Water, evoking the feeling of very deep, dark, and cold energies. There is a sense of withdrawal, descent, and of something profound. But there is also danger here and great difficulty.

YOUNGEST SON The Chinese name is Ken – the Mountain. Just as the tall mountain rests upon the earth, a solid Yang line is supported by two Yin lines, denoting the support that the young son, like the youngest daughter, receives from the rest of the family. The quality here is one of inner stillness, tranquillity, and meditation – a source of great strength for the family in time of future need.

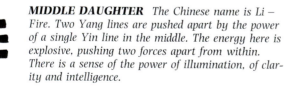

MOTHER The Chinese name is K'un – the Earth. Here we have the full power of Yin, represented by three broken lines. This is the immense energy of the earth, able to sustain all forms of life. This energy is expansive, fertile, and tolerant. It brings with it the quality of acceptance and of natural responsiveness. Here we have the power to nourish, sustain, and adapt.

The eight directions

The eight trigrams also represent the eight directions. Although North is traditionally placed at the bottom in Feng Shui charts, it is the same as magnetic North. Think of the directions as if you were looking at them from the opposite side of the compass.

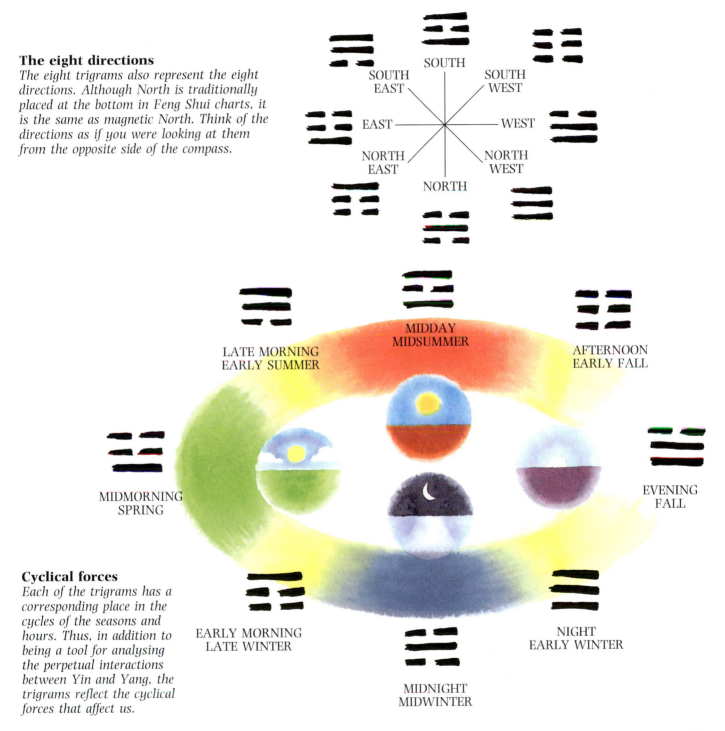

SOUTH

SOUTH EAST

SOUTH WEST

EAST — WEST

NORTH EAST

NORTH WEST

NORTH

MIDDAY MIDSUMMER

LATE MORNING EARLY SUMMER

AFTERNOON EARLY FALL

MIDMORNING SPRING

EVENING FALL

EARLY MORNING LATE WINTER

NIGHT EARLY WINTER

MIDNIGHT MIDWINTER

Cyclical forces

Each of the trigrams has a corresponding place in the cycles of the seasons and hours. Thus, in addition to being a tool for analysing the perpetual interactions between Yin and Yang, the trigrams reflect the cyclical forces that affect us.

25

The dragon-horse and tortoise

Numbers have a profound significance in Feng Shui. Just as Chinese scholars could trace the progression of changes from the unity of Wu Chi to the multiplicity that flows from the hexagrams of the I Ching, so their unfolding understanding of the natural world led them to a closer study of numbers and their significance. Their analysis and conclusions are today generally embraced by the term "numerology" – a field of study essential for the Feng Shui practitioner.

Numerology has its origins in the legendary past, when much of China was submerged by a great flood. Stricken villagers reported seeing a horse with a dragon's head emerging from the flood waters. Then came a second flood, said by some to have taken place about 6000 years ago. A tortoise with distinctive markings on its shell was seen in the River Lo. The markings on both the fabled dragon-horse and the tortoise were held to represent universal principles that govern all the manifestations of the universe.

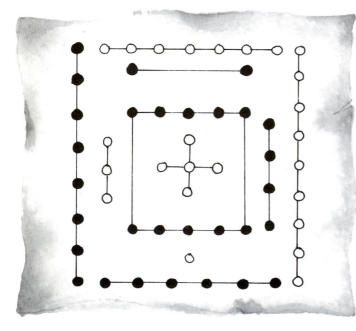

The horse's markings
On the horse's side were a series of markings that were recorded for posterity as a radiating set of squares (left). If you count up each of the lines, you will find each of the numerals from one to nine, with a square configuration numbering five in the middle.

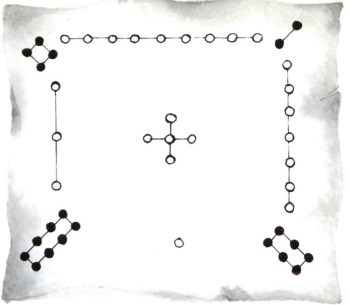

The tortoise's markings
The markings on the tortoise's back were recorded in this traditional diagram (right).

The Chinese number box
The markings on the dragon-horse and tortoise were then converted to make the now-famous Chinese number box (below right) in which the numbers added in any direction total 15. This was held to reflect the harmony of the forces of Yin and Yang, and therefore of the universe.

4	9	2
3	5	7
8	1	6

The numbers and their positions
Study of the markings on the dragon-horse and tortoise reveals certain common features: the number three is on the left, the number five is at the centre and so forth. In Chinese numerology, the position and relationship of each of the numbers to each other has a significance which is used to analyze or predict a wide range of phenomena: a person's health, job, marriage, and finances as well as their future and the web of their human relationships. In Feng Shui, each number denotes a point on the compass: the bottom centre (number 1) is North; the top center is South (number 9). The full relationship is shown on the next page.

Numbers and trigrams

Once the basic formulas of the patterns of change were established though the trigrams, they could be married with the sequence of numbers to create various significant arrangements. The first arrangement, usually termed simply "The First Sequence" or "The Sequence of Earlier Heaven", was a perfect balance of forces. Each of the opposites was placed across from its partner in a circle.

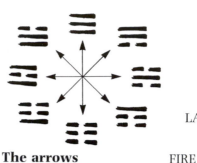

The arrows
These indicate the pairs of interacting opposites in "The Sequence of Earlier Heaven".

The names
"The Sequence of Earlier Heaven", showing the names of the trigrams.

The numbers
These correspond to each of the trigrams in "The Sequence of Earlier Heaven".

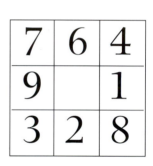

7	6	4
9	1	1
3	2	8

The Sequence of Earlier Heaven
This sequence shows the energetic forces that express themselves at every moment, but it is, in a sense, a lifeless diagram. The sequence is perfectly stable and balanced. It depicts the forces but does not show how they interact or lead to motion. For example, Heaven is perfectly balanced by Earth, and Fire by Water. Thus, the energy of will power (Heaven) is perfectly poised in relation to the capacity of acceptance (Earth). The explosive force of Fire is balanced by the descending energy of Water. Similarly, the fresh energies of the Lake are held in check by the stillness of the Mountain; the gentle power of the Wind restrains the potential force of the Thunder. This arrangement is like a still life. Feng Shui practitioners refer to it as "The Tools": it shows the patterns of energy, but not how they move and work.

The Sequence of Later Heaven

Now we can see the full display of the energies acting as a cycle, below, unlike the preceding static design. This model is sometimes known as "King Wen's Arrangement" or "The Sequence of Later Heaven". Now the tools are at work. This is the same as the configuration of trigrams showing the cycles of seasons and the transmutation of day into night (see pp. 24-5). It is a living model of the constant progression of birth, decay, and creation.

To read the sequence correctly, you begin at that point on the circumference of the circle where Yin changes to Yang. Here you find the creative force rising, expressed by the full strength of the three Yang lines of the trigram Heaven. In the sequence of the seasons, this is early Winter, the onset of the season of deepest concentration.

Moving around 45 degrees to the left, at the bottom of the circle, is Midwinter, whose trigram is Water: profound, dark, and difficult, the ground of creation. Then comes the energy of the Mountain, the stillness of late Winter, the transition to new growth. Spring emerges like the explosive force of Thunder, the irresistible power of all nature. Everything that comes forth in the Spring must then fulfil its pattern of growth, requiring patient, prolonged work. This is

the power of the early Summer, whose trigram is Wind – gentle, persistent, and pervasive. The energy of Midsummer is symbolized by the trigram for Fire, in which everything is startlingly illuminated and seen in the fullness of its powers.

The intensity of Summer completes its work in the fruition of Fall, beginning with the trigram Earth and reaching its culmination in the trigram of the Lake. This brings us to the depths of Fall and the decay of the year, the fullest extent of Yin, out of which Yang is again born. Thus, the vision of the I Ching is of a vast, revolving cascade of energy, not a linear world in which death is the end of life. At the farthest point of the cycle we are not at an end but at a beginning.

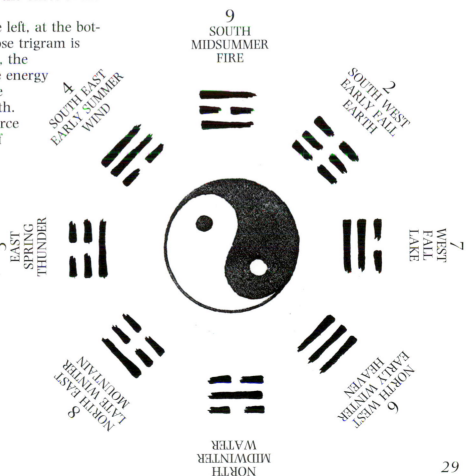

9
SOUTH
MIDSUMMER
FIRE

4
SOUTH EAST
EARLY SUMMER
WIND

2
SOUTH WEST
EARLY FALL
EARTH

3
EAST
SPRING
THUNDER

7
WEST
FALL
LAKE

8
NORTH EAST
LATE WINTER
MOUNTAIN

6
NORTH WEST
EARLY WINTER
HEAVEN

1
NORTH
MIDWINTER
WATER

29

The contours of time

Time is the curve of the universe. It is the recurrent pattern of the unfolding cosmos. "To master change, nothing is more important than to understand time," says the Taoist *Book of Balance and Harmony*.

The observations of the earliest Feng Shui practitioners and the experience of those who have developed the art down to the present day led them to perceive cycles of time recurring over different durations. The largest cycle they could detect had a total span of 180 years. This comprised nine cycles of 20 years, which then repeated themselves in sequence at the end of each of the nine 20-year periods. Within each 20-year cycle were the smaller cycles of the years, months, days, hours, and seconds. Each of these cycles continues to be used in Feng Shui for understanding and predicting the behaviour of energy.

The shortest cycles, those that take place in less than one year, are normally used for advising people who are planning special events such as marriages, the signing of contracts, and the opening of new buildings, offices, and shops. The aim is to determine on which day of a particular month (or even which hours on that day) are best for moving into a new house or undertaking a major business commitment.

The longer rhythms are taken into account in making decisions about major life changes, such as

Time and energy
As the earth turns around the sun the solar energy strikes each point on the earth at different angles and in different locations each day. Feng Shui practitioners must take into account both the changing influence of the sun and the timing and direction of all other known influences.

changing careers. These cycles begin with the lunar year. The phases of the moon form the basis of the Chinese calendar (see facing page) and the year normally begins at a point in early February.

Each year, on the professional advice of Feng Shui experts, countless owners and occupants make significant physical alterations to their homes and offices. This is most common in Chinese communities, but increasingly the practice is becoming more widespread. The changes range from repainting the walls and repositioning furniture, mirrors, and decorations through to adjusting the alignment of doors and partitions. Whether the changes are small or large, all are done to take into account the way in which the energetic environment changes with the various cycles of time.

Beyond the annual cycle, there is a larger pattern of change that occurs over 20 years. This corresponds to the system of numerology, and the significance of each of the nine basic numerals. Each number is related to a location (see p. 29). Knowing this, Feng Shui practitioners are able to warn their clients about the possible qualities of energy that will affect them in specific directions in specific years. The sequence of boxes (right) trace the movement of a particular aspect of energy through the nine years, from 1995 to 2003.

The dark boxes indicate the direction from which harmful energy may be expected or the area where one should be particularly careful.

The cycles of time
The progression of changes: one second, one hour, one day, one month, one year, 20 years, 180 years.

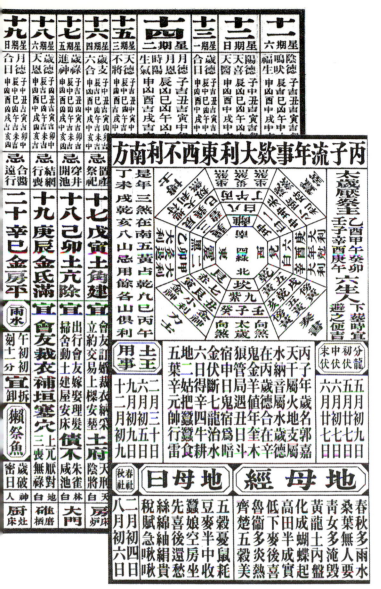

The Chinese calendar

The earliest Chinese calendars were drawn up by the astrologers of the Imperial Court. A Chinese calendar resembles an almanac, originally giving topical advice to farmers as they planned their agricultural year. Today, a Chinese calendar includes a wider range of information. The calendar in front covers a single year. Instead of giving the days and dates, the top line tells the principal direction from which positive energy can be expected throughout the year. Below that is a hexagon, constructed according to the eight trigrams. That is further subdivided to give 24 different directions: the calendar tells the impact of the energy coming from each angle. The bottom half of the calendar gives important advice on the appropriate times for burials and the orientation of grave sites according to the movement of energy that year.

The calendar behind starts at the top with the dates and days of the week. Below that is the name and expected time of the particular energy that will be most beneficial on that date. Then comes advice on activities that should be avoided on that day. This is followed by a row of characters giving the correspondences between the day and the lunar calendar, the Five Energies, and the stars. The last three rows give further advice, including activities that are particularly recommended for that day.

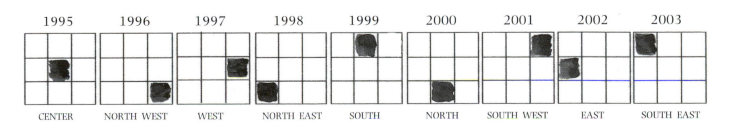

1995	1996	1997	1998	1999	2000	2001	2002	2003
CENTER	NORTH WEST	WEST	NORTH EAST	SOUTH	NORTH	SOUTH WEST	EAST	SOUTH EAST

The Five Energies

There are five fundamental movements of energy. Forces that move outward and inward, rise and descend, and rotate. The study of these movements forms the basis of one of the most famous systems in all Chinese wisdom, dating back to at least the third century BCE and possibly much earlier. It is most commonly known as "The Theory of the Five Elements". This theory, however, is essentially a study of the movement of energy, rather than a method for cataloguing "elements". It is one of the essential tools of the Feng Shui practitioner precisely because of its focus on the energetic qualities of our world.

The five movements of energy are commonly known by the names of five phenomena, which symbolize all other energetic movements of the same type: Fire, Earth, Metal, Water, and Wood.

Associated with each of these Five Energies are various qualities or vibrations that we experience every day – colors, smells, and tastes. They correspond with seasons, foods, directions, and numbers. The system has also been used extensively in traditional Chinese medicine, both for the diagnosis of conditions and for herbal, acupuncture, and other treatments. Each of the internal organs and the twelve principal meridians, or energy pathways, of the body is classified according to one of The Five Energies.

All these vibrations interact with each other in cyclical patterns. We see this most clearly in the rotation of the seasons. Energy expands outward in the Spring, giving rise to the upward power of energy in Summer. It then begins to condense inward in the Fall and sink downward in Winter. The cycle begins again with the expansion of Spring. So it is perpetually rising, expanding, condensing, and descending, with a period of transition, when the energy direction changes from one phase to another. This constant force of transition is the horizontally rotating energy of Earth.

	FIRE	EARTH	METAL	WATER	WOOD
SEASON	Summer	Transition between seasons	Fall	Winter	Spring
DIRECTION	South	Center	West	North	East
NUMBERS	9	2,5,8	6,7	1	3,4
COLOR	Red	Yellow	White	Blue/Black	Green
TASTE	Bitter	Sweet	Pungent	Salty	Sour
SMELL	Scorched	Fragrant	Rotten	Putrid	Rancid
ORGAN	Heart	Stomach	Lung	Kidney	Liver

Fire energy shoots upward. This is the pattern of energy when the cycle is at its peak. It is the Summer of the year or the phase of the full moon, brilliant and full. Once Fire energy is at its maximum, it will begin to diminish and seek rest.

Wood symbolizes energy that expands in all directions. This energy has great force, growing outward like a tree. This is the phase of the cycle in which things emerge and begin to grow. It is the waxing moon, the power to give birth, the power of Spring.

Earth energy moves horizontally around its own axis, affecting the period of change between each season. This movement is sometimes shown as the central point of the Five Energies, sometimes as the phase between the upward movement of Fire and the inward movement of Metal. It is the moon before it wanes – large, golden, full.

Water's energy descends. This is the phase in the cycle at which things reach their point of maximum rest and concentration. It is the new moon, dark and about to give birth. It is the Winter of the year.

Metal, being the most dense of all energy forms is produced by the movement of energy inward. It has a condensing, coagulating quality. It is the waning moon, the Fall of the year.

33

The cycles of change

The Five Energies change in a natural progression from one to the other. This is known as The Creative Cycle. Each energy is preceded by another, known as its parent. Thus each of the five directions of energy is the parent of the movement which follows it and the child of the movement that precedes it. When you study the cycles on these pages, it is important to remember that, like scientific formulas, they are symbolic representations of the interaction of energy.

In The Creative Cycle of the Five Energies, Fire is the parent of Earth. It is out of the heat of full summer (Fire) that the tranquil mildness of late summer (Earth) comes. The upward force of Fire naturally calls forth the pull of Earth's gravity.

Earth is the parent of Metal. It is from the powerful, rotating movement of Earth that the contracting motion of Metal condenses.

Metal is the parent of Water. Out of the contraction of energy symbolized by Metal develops the downward movement symbolized by Water. The descent of Water energy derives its momentum from the condensing action of Metal.

Water is the parent of Wood. The downward force of energy (Water) creates the momentum that then expresses itself as the creative, expansive force of Wood energy.

Wood, in turn, is the parent of Fire. It is from the expansive, bursting power of Wood that the forceful upward rush of Fire finally explodes. In the Control Cycle, the Five Energies control the intensity and influence of each other (see facing page).

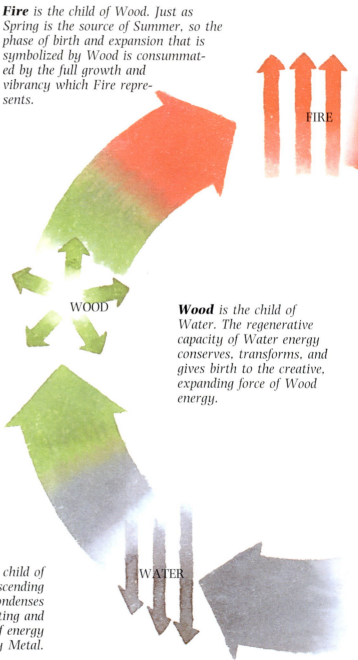

Fire is the child of Wood. Just as Spring is the source of Summer, so the phase of birth and expansion that is symbolized by Wood is consummated by the full growth and vibrancy which Fire represents.

FIRE

WOOD

Wood is the child of Water. The regenerative capacity of Water energy conserves, transforms, and gives birth to the creative, expanding force of Wood energy.

Water is the child of Metal. The descending energy of Water condenses out of the contracting and inward movement of energy symbolized by Metal.

WATER

THE CONTROL CYCLE

Earth is the child of Fire. When The Creative Cycle of the Five Energies reaches the peak of its movement, the energy blazes upward (Fire). And, as with all rhythmic, wave-like motion, it is out of this ascending movement that the power to return is born.

EARTH

Metal is the child of Earth. It is out of the action of the Earth energy that the contracting movement of Metal is born. If Metal energy is weak, it may be because it is not being nourished by its parent, Earth.

METAL

Fire controls Metal. The rising and warming force of Fire energy keeps the contracting and closing movement of Metal ener-gy from compressing and solidifying. If Fire is weak, Metal becomes rigid. If Fire is too powerful, Metal is not able to focus inward and loses form.

Wood controls Earth. The movement of Earth energy is prevented from closing in on itself or slowing to a stop by the influence of the expanding, growth energy of Wood. If Wood is weak, Earth becomes sluggish. If Wood is too strong, it disturbs Earth.

Water controls Fire. The upward rush of Fire energy is balanced by the opposite downward pull of water. If Water energy is weak, Fire blazes up. If Water is too strong, it may extinguish Fire.

Earth controls Water. The descending and sinking pull of the Water energy is restrained by the centripetal pull of the rotating Earth energy. If Earth is weak, Water sinks deeper. If Earth is too strong, it impedes the natural movement of Water.

Metal controls Wood. The outward-moving energy of Wood is balanced by the opposite, contracting, and inward movement of Metal. If Metal is weak, the effect of Wood may become excessive. If Metal is overpowering, it may harm Wood.

35

The world of form

Places and buildings have color and shape. Both these aspects have an energetic quality. As we have seen, specific colors are associated with The Five Energies. Even without studying anything about this, we know that we have a natural, intuitive response to color. Nowadays, it is common to explain our response to color by referring to the vibrating energy of the electromagnetic spectrum, but the essential response of the human organism to the energy of different colors has been known and studied for countless years. You can easily imagine the difference, for example, between cooking in a kitchen painted in black, or in warm yellow. Your response is more than a question of personal preference, although the color you feel most comfortable with in that context could tell the Feng Shui practitioner much about you!

Shapes, too, have a particular energetic quality, affecting the flow of energies within them and around them. As with color, we respond differently to angularity and to roundness – and our responses will vary according to the conditions and circumstances in which we encounter any particular shape. In the theory of The Five Energies, specific shapes are associated with Fire, Earth, Metal, Water, and Wood. When it comes to painting or choosing construction materials, the selection of color is important to ensure the overall harmony of the various energies.

Round shapes
A round structure, such as a water tower or geodesic dome, has the energetic quality of Metal. Its energy is directed inward. Such structures will function most harmoniously if they are of the color associated with Metal: white.

Square shapes
A square shape denotes Earth. This is a common shape for many homes, either with flat roofs or ones that slope very gently. The shape itself expresses the supportive, secure, and stable quality of Earth. Warm tones of yellow and brown are ideal.

Curving, horizontal shapes

A building that has a curving or indented, horizontal shape is expressive of the flowing and constantly changing aspect of Water energy. Such buildings are best constructed of dark materials or painted in the dark blues or black of Water energy.

Triangular shapes

The inspiring, exciting upward rush of Fire energy makes the triangle the shape for buildings such as temples or other places of worship. The color most perfectly suited to such structures is red. For example, the red brick and stone that is common on certain churches, and the brilliant red paintwork on the pillars of many oriental places of worship.

Rectangular shapes

Buildings that have a strong rectangular shape express growth, expansiveness, and power. This is typical of Wood energy. Shades of green are best suited to them, including green-tinted glass.

The Five Animals

Human beings are always seeking harmony on a physical and psychological level. To bring our lives and environment into harmony Feng Shui practitioners rely on several distinctive mental maps in order to interpret daily events. These serve as the underlying assumptions used to determine even such commonplace affairs as the arrangement of furniture in the home.

As with Yin and Yang, the eight trigrams, and The Five Energies (see pp. 16-29), Feng Shui principles can be depicted and used almost like a navigational map – with one crucial difference. On the Feng Shui map the location of the human being at any moment determines the directions and relationships of the rest of the surrounding world.

One of the most common maps (see Part Two) is known simply as "The Five Animals". At first glance it appears to have a mythical quality, but you can use it as a template to help you understand and assess a remarkable range of phenomena from the physical layout of a dwelling, through to the dynamics of teamwork, or the functioning of dynamic forces in the human personality.

The Feng Shui starting point is the direction in which the speaker is facing. On the template (see facing page) an alert snake occupies the center, facing forward. A dragon is on its left (the Chinese call their left side their "dragon side"), a tiger on the right, a phoenix in front, and a tortoise behind.

Originally, each animal had certain attributes. The tortoise was in the relative position North. Its color black, its season Winter, its element Water. The dragon was to the East; its color green, its season Spring, its element Wood. The phoenix was to the South, associated with red, Summer, and Fire. The tiger's attributes were the West, white, Fall, and Metal. At the center was the snake, yellowy brown, the color of Earth, and the pivot around which the seasons turned.

The tortoise
Equipped with an immensely strong shell, the tortoise is characterized by stability. It conveys a sense of great security. Its proper position is at the back, where, like a shell, it provides security, longevity, and freedom from the fear of attack from the rear.

The dragon

The dragon is a creature unseen in the natural world. Like the phoenix, it is far-sighted and possesses a spiritual quality. The dragon receives the information gathered by the bird, reflects upon it, and makes important decisions. Although it soars above the ground, the dragon is typically depicted resting in the clouds, a figure of stability. It has amazing power and symbolizes the wisdom aspect of the mind.

The phoenix

A mythical bird that never dies, the phoenix flies far ahead to the front, always scanning the landscape and distant space. It represents our capacity for vision, for collecting sensory information about our environment and the events unfolding within it. The phoenix, with its great beauty, creates intense excitement and deathless inspiration.

The snake

Coiled at the center, alert, stable, and ready to act in a flash, the snake is protected by the four outlying creatures, but is also able to direct them. Like the general of an army, it receives information from all directions and is able to draw on the special qualities of the forces at its command to take timely and wise action.

The tiger

Evoking physical strength and violence, the tiger can both defend and attack. It is essential for survival, but must be carefully controlled. Ready to spring forward on our right side, it is always ready to detect the presence of any threat. But it also represents the danger of violence within our nature.

The fields and forces

The universe is a vast field of energy. The study of Feng Shui is the study of that energy.

The entire cosmos is a shimmering net of constant communication. Vibrations move through this web of energy at inconceivable speed. Distant tremors set up correspondences in bodies and events apparently separated by light years. Although our senses seem to perceive a world of separate forms, whatever we experience is a spectrum of vitality.

To talk about the cosmos as an energetic spectrum is quite commonplace among today's late-twentieth century scientists. But it was a fundamental tenet of Chinese science well before the start of this millennium.

"All substance and form is energy. It is yin and yang, the motion of the sun, moon and stars, everything that emerges and dissolves. It is the clouds, the mist, the fog and moisture. The heart of all living beings, all growth and development is energy," wrote the Chinese philosopher and naturalist, Lu Yen, often known affectionately as Ancestor Yu.

Chih

Chung

The original Chinese phrase that expressed our relationship to the rest of the universe was Chih Chung (*left*). It is often translated as magnetism. The exploration of attractions of all sorts led early Chinese scientists in the Later Han Empire, just over 2000 years ago, to identify specific magnetic polarities. Their work has been described as "the greatest Chinese contribution to physics". By T'ang times (618-906 CE) a compass was in use. But the sense in which it was originally used went far beyond the limited meaning of magnetism in modern science.

Through similar, careful observations, which were forming the basis of Chinese medicine, it became clear that the human body, too, had magnetic properties (as latter-day scientists have established through the presence of iron in the blood). Our bodies are part of and affected by the earth's magnetic field, and each of us has an energetic field extending beyond the body's visible limits (*below*).

The energetic imprint of each human being is determined by the configuration of the force field of the universe at any one moment. This understanding lies at the very heart of Feng Shui. Authentic Feng Shui does not consist of a series of fixed rules about when to do things or where to put objects. Instead, it relies on a deep understanding of the patterns of energy in the universe and their interaction with each individual. In order to advise an individual a Feng Shui practitioner must take into account that person's birth time, the influence of near and distant galaxies (*right*), and the celestial rhythms that embrace us all.

The movement of energy

Energy moves. That is its inherent nature. Whether the Feng Shui practitioner is observing the forces of Yin and Yang, the modulations of the I Ching, the cycles of The Five Energies, or the behaviour of energy in your home, all is in motion. Ordinarily our senses perceive the most obvious forms of motion – traffic passing by in the street or the cool rush of the wind against the skin. We are less conscious of the subtle movements of energy as it passes invisibly through the space of an open room or the vibration of the patterns of energy in the walls and furnishings.

Subtle movements of energy are unfolding all the time. We are immersed in them and experience them, whether awake or asleep. We feel uneasy, restless, or impatient when we sit in one corner of a room. We change chairs to sit in another corner; for some reason we find it more refreshing or more tranquil. We go to someone's home, perhaps for a party; instinctively we avoid standing by an open doorway and seek another part of the room. Countless moments like this in our everyday lives arise from our inherent awareness of the energies in our environment.

Invisible designs

Our experience of the movement of energy varies. Suppose we are in a warm room and it is cold outside. We open a window on one side of the room and open the door on the other side. The cold air surges straight through. We can literally feel it and breathe it. But we cannot see it. It is an invisible design that weaves its way through the space of our room.

It could be misleading to think of all energetic patterns simply as wind rushing through. If we take the analogy with the wind too far, then, when we think we feel nothing happening in the air, we may tend to assume that there are no energy movements going on. But as the drawings on these pages show, there are currents of energy in motion all the time.

In most circumstances, the natural tendency of energy is to circulate in a series of curves, sometimes sweeping around a room in a single wave, sometimes more forcefully spinning through the space.

Circulating energy
As energy enters this room (right), it fills the entire doorway. It moves through the room, making a lazy circle around the whole area before moving on. A person sitting in the path of the entering energy will feel a subtle sense of disturbance and will probably not be at ease. On the other hand, a person sitting in the corner that is foremost in the drawing may sense that the area is somehow lifeless, since the current of energy bypasses them.

Revolving energies
As energies enter the room they may start to revolve before passing through.

Rotating energy
A strong field of energy may rotate around the room like a spinning top.

43

Entrances and exits

A door opposite a window

If a door is directly opposite a window (left), energy that enters the room will normally pass straight through and out the other side. Anyone sitting in its path will probably feel continual disturbance. Anyone occupying the areas away from the door or window may sense dullness or emptiness around them. If the window and door are both open, the current of energy will be very strong. If the window is closed but not blocked off, some energy will continue to move through the glass, as light does. If the door is closed, the window shuttered, or the curtains drawn, then the transit of energy will be blocked.

One entry and exit

In this room (right), which has no window and only one door, there is only one entry and exit point for the current of energy. The energy returns to the original point of entry, creating constant confusion and competition between the energetic forces near the doorway.

Two entry or exit points
Here (left) the position of the door and window permits the energy to circulate calmly, but only in part of the room. Moving in a characteristic curve, the energy enters the room through either the door or window and moves around the periphery of the space, seeking a way out. A person sitting at the mid-point of this smooth trajectory will experience subtle refreshment because of the gentle circulation, but a person on the other side of the room may sense a lack of vitality in the air, because the flow of energy bypasses them.

Three entry or exit points
Energy entering this room (right) has three entry or exit points, whether doors or windows, to choose from. Together they influence the way energy circulates. It flows in through the main entry point. Some of it circles around and leaves by the nearest exit. Some makes a full circle of the room and leaves through the exit on the farthest side from the door. The most beneficial location in this room is a corner, ideal for the main sitting area, although the energy flow in most of the room is already harmonious.

45

Energy flow in the bedroom

Your bedroom is a field of energy. Even objects that appear to be still are in motion. Thus your bedroom, like any place on the planet, is constituted of internal vibrations from the condensed energy of matter and the movement of energetic waves through space. Both these manifestations of energy influence each other and affect anyone in the room.

Think of your bedroom as being like a stream. The walls, ceiling, floor, and furniture are the living banks of the stream. The space is the water that fills the stream. The current is the energetic force that moves through the stream, interacting with the living energy of the banks of the stream. For example, if you place your bed under a protruding beam in the ceiling, as in the illustration below, the energy of the beam will influence the pattern of the invisible energy that is constantly moving in the room. It creates an invisible downward deflection of pressure on to your torso while you sleep. The pressure on your chest will inhibit your breathing, which is one of the fundamental "Wind" movements of your body.

A series of beams

Some homes have a series of beams across the bedroom ceiling (right). This creates a multiple ripple effect in the descending energy patterns and can create considerable disturbance in the "silent winds" of the room. The downward pressure from each beam is like a series of hammer blows. If your bed is underneath, they rain down on you in constantly, one by one. A flat ceiling is definitely preferable so consider using another room for your bedroom.

Overhead beam

Night after night, the overhead beam (left) sets up a constant disturbance of your breath as you lie beneath it. This subtle influence will have a sustained impact on your sleep and therefore disturb your resting mind. Your long-term health will be affected. Try to find a way to move your bed so that it is clear of the beam.

A pointed or sloping roof

In a room under a roof like this (left), the internal streams of energy bounce around like balls on a billiard table. This type of room can have a stimulating effect for brief periods so can be used as a child's playroom. But as a bedroom you would be trying to sleep in a constant, random fluctuation of energetic forces. Nor is it a room which you should use for sustained thought or for meditation. The room would be better used as a loft for storage.

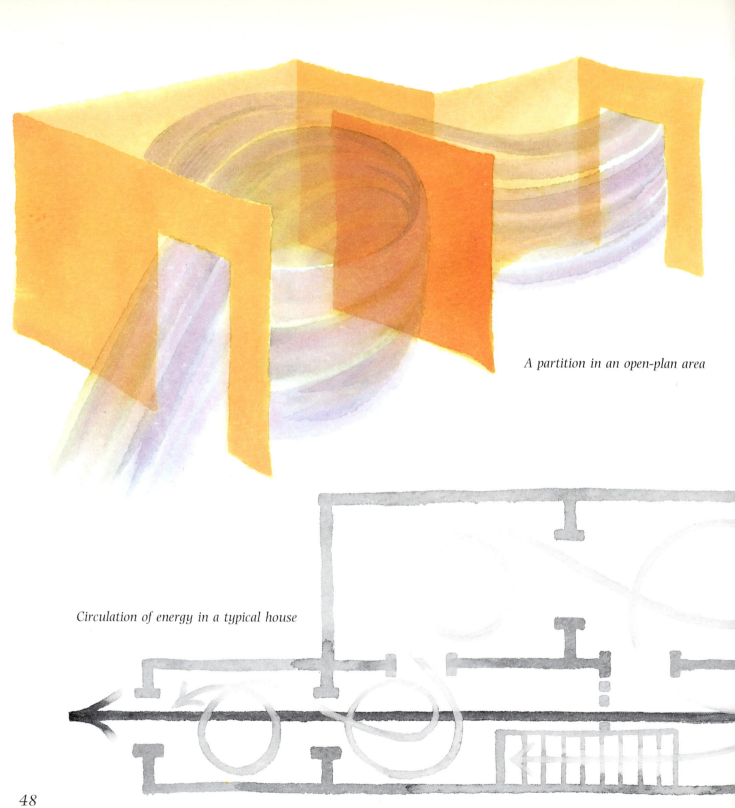

A partition in an open-plan area

Circulation of energy in a typical house

The moving stream

In ancient scroll paintings from China, sages are often drawn sitting by mountain streams or river banks. In such places there is much to learn about the movement of energy in all its forms.

For example, the drawing at the top of the facing page shows what happens if a partition is constructed in an open-plan area. In this case, the energy originally entered the room through the main door, rushed straight through the space, and left by the back door. The rest of the room was bypassed, leaving the area toward the front door virtually stagnant. When the partition was inserted, just like a small breakwater in a stream, the flow of energy changed. Now there is a full circle taking in the whole of the front area of the room. The presence of the partition has also slowed the energy down so that it is more gentle throughout.

What happens to energy as it tries to move through a complex configuration of rooms? The floor plan (*bottom left*) shows the ground floor of a typical house, with stairs going up to the second floor. Originally, there was a clear passage from the front door straight through to the back door. Energy entering the front went straight out the back. This is represented by the straight arrow. The effect was to deprive the two main rooms on the ground floor of any possible benefit from the energy and to create a forceful stream pulsing through the back room. If, as in many homes, the back room was used as a kitchen, anyone working there for several hours might become agitated and confused, as if standing in a perpetual draft.

New circulation

To solve these problems, a partition was constructed to close off the open hallway just beside the doorway leading into the large room at the front of the house. On the floor plan this is represented by the small dotted line across the hallway. Now the energy is diverted into the front room, where it circles around and finds the outlet into the rear room. It then circles around again in the rear room until it passes out into the passageway behind the stairs. It makes a further coil before drifting into the back room, makes a final lazy loop and then heads out the back door. Some of the original energy slips upstairs, but the main circulation remains on the ground floor.

A gentle stream

From this example, we can see the difference that the application of Feng Shui principles makes to a home. What may have seemed originally to have been a perfectly normal architectural design created two major problems for a living environment. There was a rush of energy perpetually disturbing the back room and completely bypassing the main living areas.

We can see the immense effect a small change can have at a critical point. The partition erected across the open hallway could be used in several ways. In the entrance hall it could be a space for hanging a decoration or a mirror, or creating a storage closet for coats. On the reverse side, it could be used for shelving, a closet, or equipment. But the main effect is to transform the original energy flow.

As a result of this single change the whole of the ground floor has become the setting for a gentle stream of energy that meanders in natural circles through all the living areas, subtly fills the entire space, and then calmly departs.

Interior arrangements

A young working couple with one child buys a small house, conveniently located within easy reach of both the husband's and wife's places of work. On the ground floor is a large sitting room that opens on to a back garden. It can also be used as a dining area. There are two bedrooms, one for the parents and a smaller one for the child. To the right of the front door is a bathroom. At the rear, near the glass doors opening on to the garden, is a small kitchen. Stairs to the upper floor are on the left of the front door as you enter.

Soon after the couple moves in, the wife receives an important promotion at work that she has been seeking for some time. A year later she is delighted when her doctor tells her she is pregnant with her second child. It has been a good year for the family's finances as well. But the family is about to grow and they decide that they need a larger home and put the property up for sale.

The house is attractive and is bought by a second couple, also with a young child. They have very different ideas about the way they want their home to look. They redecorate the interior, taking the opportunity to buy themselves new furniture. Unfortunately, within a year and a half of moving in, the husband injures himself at work and is laid off. Money becomes a constant source of argument at home. To make matters worse things start to go wrong in the house, first with the electrical wiring and later the plumbing. All these mishaps come along one after the other; there does not appear to be any connection between them.

If the second couple were to call in a Feng Shui expert, he would be very interested in the story of the differing fortunes of the two families. He might conclude that the energy originally concentrated in the area of the house had been positive, but that over time the energetic configuration had changed. Or he might conclude that the energy had remained constant but that the second couple was not living in harmony with it. If he were to examine the home, he would be very interested in the way in which the second couple redecorated it and arranged their new furniture.

How the couples used the space
The two drawings on the facing page show the ways in which both families used the space in the same house. Each of the changes introduced by the second family, seen through the eyes of the Feng Shui expert, caused a problem. The first couple had a large floor-to-ceiling bookcase creating a decorative partition to separate off the sitting area from the entrance, and placed their sofa against the wall, opposite the television. The second couple liked looking straight out to the garden and put their new sofa and chairs in the middle of the open space with the back toward the front door. This meant that their major sitting area was exposed to a direct current from the front door through to the garden and that they positioned themselves in the middle of this, with no support at their backs.

The second couple liked the open-plan layout they had created. They kept the door of the kitchen permanently open and, except when in use, left the door of the small bathroom ajar. This meant that the central area of the home was constantly exposed to odors and energies from which it had previously been protected, since the first couple kept these doors closed.

There are two other differences. The second couple put the beds in both bedrooms opposite the doors so that they and their child could easily see out into the main area. This also exposed both beds to the direct currents of energy entering the rooms through the doorways, and particularly in the case of the child, to the current passing straight through to the window over the head of the bed. In the bedrooms arranged by the second couple, the mirror on the dressing table and the wall mirror in the

FIRST COUPLE

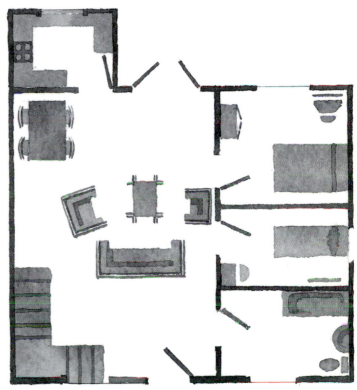

SECOND COUPLE

child's room face the beds; the mirrors did not face the beds when the first family lived there.

All these differences could affect the harmony of the home, the lives of the people in it, and the energetic forces around the home. If the Feng Shui expert had met the second couple at the house he would have immediately noticed that their new furniture was metallic and that they had painted the interior light grey. It was a very cold internal environment. The fortunate first couple had deep red coverings on the furniture in the sitting area and a soft rose tint on the walls.

Caves and cities

The places where we spend our lives are part of our existence. Where we are is part of what determines who we are. Our locations have a profound influence on us. We, in turn, transform them. Every time we find a home, move to a new office, or choose a place to sit in a crowded room, we make a decision and have to live with its consequences. Our location influences what happens to us at any moment, just as surely as standing under a tree in a thunderstorm increases the chances of our being struck by lightning.

Protection at the back, water in front
From caves in the mountains to great capitals of commerce, humanity has selected sites that offered physical protection to the rear and access to waterways in the front. Hong Kong is poised between the South China Sea and the Central Mountains of China, New York between the Appalachians and the Atlantic, London between the Chilterns and the River Thames. All these cities are great contemporary centers of communication and finance.

As you will see from the history of Feng Shui (see pp. 58-61), our ancestors experimented with different ways of finding shelter and living on this planet. The principles of Feng Shui are based on that accumulated experience.

From what we know of the earliest human habitation, there is much in the experience of cave dwellers that remains true today. Living and sleeping in the open is hazardous and offers no protection against the elements. Camping under trees or living in a hole in the ground offers little shelter and can be fatal in storms. A cave offers more protection, and acts like a shell or backbone, preventing access from the rear. We remain vulnerable at the front, however, but can erect a barrier in front of our living area. To have a secure outdoor area for communal activities would also be important and we need access to drinking water if we are to remain alive. Either we need to live by a stream or a river or the area must be suitable for digging wells. Living near a river has another advantage: it acts as an added line of defence, just as medieval moats were used to defend castles.

We can see the concept of "wind" and "water" emerging from this description of the fundamental needs of a good location. The water is in front. But where is the wind? It stirs the air between the water and the cave entrance. The movement of the river freshens the air and there is a cleanness and vigour in the wind as it brushes the hillsides or mountain slopes.

Today, of course, very few people dwell in caves or are camped by the sides of rivers. But the fundamental experience of people trying to find good locations for human habitation remain in our collective memory. They have influenced the location of cities and the sites of ancestral homes. They are used to this day by Feng Shui practitioners when advising people on houses and offices even in metropolitan cities.

Finding your spot

The importance of Wind and Water applies not only to the location of large centers of human habitation. Your home and your office are habitations also and you find yourself naturally concerned about the environments in which you spend so much of your lifetime. When you choose a house or apartment you worry about the price you will pay, the cost of living in the area, and the convenience of the location. But you also want to know about the neighbourhood. You are concerned about the atmosphere of the locality: you want to know how quiet it is, whether it is safe, whether the air is oppressive. You want to know what effect living there will have on you.

In order to answer this question, the Feng Shui practitioner takes many aspects into account. It is not just a question of whether you like the house or apartment. The various Feng Shui principles are used. What is the balance of Yin and Yang (see pp. 18-23)? How does the alignment of the home fit with the sequence of trigrams in the I Ching? Is it an appropriate location in view of the magnetic and other forces and the relevant cycles of time? Does the overall configuration of the home and neighbouring buildings correspond to the map of The Five Animals (see pp. 38-9)?

No location is permanently good or bad. To say that would violate the fundamental fact of change in the universe. All the converging – and changing – forces have to be taken into account. What is an appropriate location for a family home for one cycle of 20 years may be most unsuitable in the next. An auspicious location for one family may be singularly catastrophic for another. Feng Shui, like any science, explores all aspects of the situation, develops general laws, and then examines how to apply these in specific circumstances.

Moving to the countryside
You want to move to the countryside. You find a charming little house with wide open fields stretching in all directions to the rear. However, the house has no open area of its own in front: the main road runs right by the front door. You hesitate about buying it – possibly the traffic will be noisy at night. You are also reacting intuitively to the fact that the location of the house violates Feng Shui principles. It is completely unprotected at the rear and has no open space in front. Unconsciously perhaps, you feel there is something vulnerable about the location.

Effects of a high-rise tower

If someone seeks planning permission to build a high-rise tower across the street from your house, you naturally object. It will block your view, cut off your access to sunlight and air, and lower the value of your home. From the Feng Shui point of view, putting the tower in front of your home would be the equivalent of blocking off the entrance of your cave and turning it around to face inward to the mountain. Your natural sense of order is turned topsy turvy and you feel you are about to be suffocated, because your biological need for air (Wind) as you face forward will be obstructed.

The Feng Shui diamond

One day a young man, who was happily married and the father of two small children, said to his wife: "This is now the third year that I have been passed over for promotion at work, and everyone looks at me as if I'm a failure."

"But you're not a failure," his wife said to him. "You have a good background, a degree, all the training you need, and you're working in a fast-moving company. Your turn for promotion will come in good time."

But promotion didn't come and the young man felt secretly obsessed with the idea that his life was stagnating. He confessed his fears to an old college friend, who jokingly remarked: "Maybe you need some Feng Shui."

The casual jibe bit deep and the young man began tracking down what he could find on the subject – some magazine articles and two books in a local bookshop. Being a computer specialist himself, he also found the Feng Shui network on the internet. Without telling his wife what he was doing, he began to make suggestions for reorganizing their home.

"I'm not too happy about that pond in the back garden," he announced one morning at breakfast. And a couple of weeks later he told her: "I think I'll rip out all those rocks from the rock garden we have out front."

Naturally his wife was more than a bit perplexed since they had both put a lot of effort into the landscaping around their home, but the young man was intent and set about the changes, all the while keeping his thoughts to himself.

Three months later, he returned from work one day with the good news that his boss had asked him about his career plans. There was going to be a structural reorganization in the company and

they were looking for experienced staff to take on new responsibilities. "Change is in the air," said the young man to himself.

A week afterward, however, he began to notice a subtle change in the atmosphere at work. He was a man to whom people were naturally drawn, but now he sensed a slight coldness and started to find it harder and harder to get his hands on information he needed. His boss, too, noticed the change: "Is there something wrong that we need to talk about?" she asked him in her perceptive way. The young man had no answer.

For the first time he had deep misgivings about dabbling in Feng Shui. "Maybe I've been like the sorcerer's apprentice," he muttered to himself, "and I've unleashed something I can't control."

His wife knew all was not well. Next day she heard him musing aloud: "Maybe we should put that pond back in the garden again."

She sat down beside him, asked what had got into his mind, and by dint of persistent questioning extracted a confession. "I'll ask my cousin, Jean, what to do," she told him. "Her new husband comes from the Far East and she told me had an uncle who knew all about this sort of thing."

"Very difficult to practise Feng Shui perfectly from a book," said the uncle, once he had been persuaded by his new niece to come over to the couple's house. "It is something you study for years." He continued: "Feng Shui is like a diamond. When you cut a jewel, you must pay attention to all the facets. They are like little mirrors, reflecting the light of the diamond. They also reflect the light of each other. If you want to bring out the brilliance of the stone, all the cuts must be harmonious."

"So was what I did wrong?" asked the worried young man.

"No," said the uncle, "a diamond is still a diamond. But if one cut is not so well made, then it affects the light coming from the rest of the facets. Nothing you did was wrong. You just need some help to complete the work on your diamond!"

Then, much to the amazement of the young couple, the uncle reached into his little bag and drew out a beautiful Lo Pan, the Feng Shui compass. Only a master is fully trained in the art of the Lo Pan. Under the careful eye of this remarkable gentleman, they went through the whole house, examining it room by room.

"You should reposition the television and the stereo system in your living room and take down that painted mask you have on display over your fireplace. You'd be better off without all those houseplants in the bedroom. Take the mirror off the wall and put it on the inside of your clothes cupboard door. Get a side table for your bed and put your reading light on it, instead of having it on the headrest of your bed."

"Finally," said the uncle, "I suggest you change the color of your front door and sleep with your head at the other end of your bed. Are you willing to do these things?"

The couple, rather overawed by the suggestions, nodded: "We'll do it."

"But not till I return," said the uncle. "You must do all this work on the correct day at the correct time. That is very important. Without the correct timing, your diamond will be like a stone in the dark. When I come back I will also bring a small crystal that I will place in your front room."

It was not the sort of advice that the couple expected and they harboured the fear that if they made these changes, their friends would quietly shun them for being superstitious.

"I thought that at first, myself," cousin Jean told them, "and I had real trouble accepting what my husband started to tell me about all this sort of thing. But really, now I see it as a kind of cultural problem. Everyone is looking at the same world and dealing with the same realities, it's just the way of seeing that is so different."

The couple decided to go ahead with the changes (and, incidentally, they were right to take the pond out of the back garden). And, as the uncle assured them, it was only a matter of weeks before things picked up.

"We feel so different in the mornings," they told Jean. "It's as though we have slept so much better and we've been having fewer arguments with the kids. Going to work seems less of a burden and the atmosphere has really improved. And now it seems like major new responsibilities – and more money – are definitely on the cards."

"I feel as though we should pay your uncle," said the young man. "I read that Feng Shui men command very large fees."

"They do," said Jean. "In fact the advice you got from my uncle was probably priceless. But I asked him if he would do me a favour, now that I've married into his family... On the other hand, if you'd like to show respect for his culture, you can make a heart-felt offering as a sign of your gratitude and put it in a little red envelope for him."

The dawn of time

The historical origins of Feng Shui stretch back to an era of human civilization that precedes all written records. It is like a great river whose source can be traced back by following the winding of its many streams and tributaries.

At the fountainhead of all Feng Shui practice lies the theory of Yin and Yang (see pp. 16-19). The concept of the two fundamental forces existed in the oral culture of China, pre-dating all written works of natural science and medical theory and therefore stretching back well over 7000 years. In the opening chapter of the Yellow Emperor's *Classic of Internal Medicine*, which dates back to between 2690 and 2590 BCE and is the earliest medical text known to humanity, the court physician tells the Emperor:

"In ancient times those people who understood the Tao patterned themselves upon the Yin and the Yang and they lived in harmony with the arts of divination."

As Taoism developed over the centuries, the importance of Yin and Yang theory in all areas of intellectual, artistic, and scientific inquiry became immense. The theory lay at the heart of most observations and reflections on life, just as it continues to do in the art of Feng Shui to this day.

The I Ching also has an extraordinarily long history. Some accounts attribute its origins to the work of legendary figures in Chinese culture. Other scholars hold the view that the fundamental principles were established in the seventh and eighth century BCE, with the book in its contemporary form being produced at the end of the Chou dynasty in the third century CE. Confucius himself, born in 522 BCE, devoted his latter years to an extensive study of the I Ching and wrote an exhaustive commentary on it.

The theory of The Five Energies is sometimes said to stretch back to the time of Tsou Yen, who is often described as the founder of Chinese scientific

thought. In *The Historical Record*, which dates back to the first century CE, Tsou Yen is described as presenting the essential ideas of the system of The Five Energies, although the concepts may well have been in circulation long before that. *The Historical Record* says of Tsou Yen:

"He examined deeply the waxing and waning of Yin and Yang, and wrote essays of more than 100,000 words about the patterns they produced.... He began with the origin of Heaven and Earth and made notations of the constant changes of The Five Energies, arranging them until each fitted into a pattern and was confirmed by historical events.

Dwelling on the earth

From the very earliest days people have sought to dwell in ways that would enable them to survive nature's powerful eruptions – floods, earthquakes, and epidemics. From patient observation of life on the planet emerged a body of theory and practice that has led through the centuries to the development of many sciences. The principles of Feng Shui have also been refined in accordance with century upon century of careful observation.

Heaven and earth

Feng Shui is a relatively modern term. The original Chinese characters used to describe what we now call Feng Shui were Ham and Yu. Ham has the meaning of getting or receiving energy from the heavenly bodies. Yu refers to connecting our earth with the galaxy. So a clear picture emerges from this very old term – an idea of the possibility and the method of experiencing and creating connections between the planet earth and the rest of the universe. To the Chinese mind, it is the human being who stands between Heaven and Earth, connecting the two. This perception goes to the very heart of the history and inner meaning of Feng Shui.

The tradition

Feng Shui began as an oral tradition and, in large measure, it has continued to be transmitted from master to student. The scope of study is considerable. There are four levels, each with subsidiary levels within them; there is no fixed system of passing through the levels – everything depends on the judgment of the master and the aptitude of the student.

Traditionally, and this is still true in the majority of cases, if a person wished to learn Feng Shui they would have to find someone who could introduce them to a Feng Shui master. This introduction would be all-important. If the master agreed, the person would be taken on as a student. For the next few years, they would simply serve the master (possibly helping out in the home or doing other tasks assigned by the master). This period was absolutely essential to enable the master to test the personal qualities of the would-be practitioner. Feng Shui has a very strict ethical code and is not taught to anyone who could use its insights or techniques to harm others.

If the master judged that the new student was worthy of instruction, a period of personal tuition would begin. The student would accompany the master during his Feng Shui work and be given essential training. By this time, the student would become almost part of the master's family and would begin to be treated in that way. Eventually, after several further years of apprenticeship as a student – it could often be at least a decade – the master might decide to accept the student as a disciple. This would depend on the emergence of a deeper bond between the two and the transmission of more profound understanding. In all respects except blood kinship, the two would accept mutual responsibility for each other and the disciple would know that he was being prepared to continue the tradition after the death of the master.

In some instances, masters who have no family or have entered a monastic tradition, will not teach at all and may only seek pupils toward the end of their lives in order to ensure continuity in the tradition. They will follow the same painstaking process of carefully testing the character of potential students and only transmitting their full insight to those they fully trust.

In recent times younger Feng Shui masters have begun to make Feng Shui more widely known. They give lectures and workshops and write articles and books. Some give short courses. This is called "opening the first door to the secret". People who are interested can step in through the door. But once inside, the actual teachings are conducted on an entirely personal basis. In this respect, the integrity of a tradition that stretches back over the centuries is still preserved today.

The Feng Shui master

In this old drawing, the Feng Shui master of the Imperial Court is seen examining a potential site. In the very earliest days of the art, it was practised exclusively in the service of the Emperor. Slowly Feng Shui evolved into a more widespread practice. It is only in this century that it has been more openly discussed and written about.

In this picture the old master, in the centre of the group of three figures, is indicated by the little box of two characters just beside his head. The other figures in the picture are his staff, two of them carrying measuring rods. To the right of the master, one of his staff is examining the Feng Shui compass, known as the Lo Pan, which is resting on a fold-up stand.

As you look at the drawing, you can test your own comprehension of some of the basic principles of Feng Shui theory. What, in this picture, is Yin and what is Yang? Where are The Five Animals? Look at the relationship of the hill to the water and the relative height of the right side of the picture and the left side (as you face it): if you were going to position a building on this site, where would you put the front door?

A painting on silk showing a view of the Summer Palace, Beijing.

PART TWO

The natural harmonies

Where you live and work

Part Two of this book deals with the Natural Harmonies. These are based on an understanding of the Fundamental Forces introduced in Part One. These Natural Harmonies have three main aspects. First is the harmony that should exist between each person and their immediate environment – their homes and offices, shops and other places of work. Second is the harmony that should exist between that immediate environment and its broader surroundings – the location and vicinity of where people's homes and places of work are situated. Third, there is the larger harmony that should exist among all the energetic forces that converge on a person in any particular environment, even from far distant energy sources within the galaxies.

Certain underlying perceptions are common to the nine aspects of Feng Shui and influence all the practical day-to-day suggestions to which you will be introduced in this part of the book:

– the energy of the universe is mutually interpenetrating
– the energy of human beings is inseparable from both their immediate environments and the energy of the galaxies
– the energy of matter is fundamentally identical to the forms of energy we associate with light, color, and visible movement

However abstract Feng Shui theory may seem, it is really another way of looking at daily life. It is not reserved for sages in idyllic settings. Nor is it a unique Chinese way of looking at the world – and you don't have to be Chinese to appreciate or grasp it. Once you understand the fundamental principles you start to see the world in a different way.

Understanding your world
The Feng Shui way of looking at the world, gives you a set of conceptual tools that can be applied in very practical ways. This is what you are presented with in Part Two. It begins with the most important aspect of your life: the place where you live. To a Feng Shui practitioner, the first thing to consider is the impact of the actual location – is your home in a safe place, somewhere that you can relax, somewhere in which the energy patterns are conducive to the life you are leading?

It then examines the essential aspects of your home, room by room. The starting point for this tour of your home is your bedroom, because you spend up to one-third of your life there. Next come the living room, kitchen, and bathroom. There is a brief look at the Feng Shui principles that apply to your garden, before moving on to examine the work environment outside your home.

The illustrations of buildings and their interiors are deliberately generalized. For example, only the key positions of a few houses are shown, rather than all the dwellings on a street. Every effort has been made to depict a variety of living styles, since the advice is meant to be applied in a wide range of situations and by people living on different continents and with very different resources at their disposal. The important things to grasp are the underlying principles so that you can apply these to your own living arrangements.

Feng Shui for business
Today, in cities ranging from Canton to Singapore and from San Francisco to Paris, more and more senior executives are calling in a Feng Shui expert (if they can find one) to advise them on major business deals.

One American businessman living in London recently surprised his associates by flying a Feng Shui master in from Hong Kong for a weekend to inspect a possible property. He decided not to buy once the site had been given the thumbs down by the Chinese expert.

The location of your business (on a busy thorough-fare, or a quiet back street) will affect who comes to your office or shop and what volume of trade you do. But that is not all. Other factors are equally important. These include the relationship to other buildings (facing sharp corners or taller buildings, and proximity to fountains are problems that a Feng Shui expert will spot), the internal arrangement (long corridors open at both ends or incorrectly placed mirrors can be detrimental to business), and the color scheme (certain colors create a subtle sense of discomfort among customer and staff).

Feng Shui experts and architects

Sometimes a Feng Shui expert will recommend a series of architectural changes to create a more harmonious configuration of energy in a major building. This is common in Hong Kong, where property developers call in a Feng Shui master first. They want to know if the location is suitable before investing, and which direction the building should face for maximum security of return on their venture. After that, they may require the architects to work closely with the Feng Shui master and to submit their designs to him. There may be a final inspection and a yearly review, since the energy in the environment can shift.

Executives who consult Feng Shui experts argue that it makes good commercial sense, even if they themselves don't understand all the inner workings of the art. After all, they say, they have made a major investment and if spending a little more to receive this type of advice reduces the risk of failure, why not do it?

The commercial difference

For example, in an increasingly competitive world many commercial centers spend huge sums on redecorating their plazas, office areas, and shops.

The services and products they offer may be of high quality yet they fail to attract business in sufficient volume. A competitor in another location, offering a comparable service or product, may spend far less on décor and bring in many more clients and customers. Often failure is blamed on poor marketing strategies, the overall financial climate, and inadequate management. All those reasons may be valid. But if the whole picture is examined through the eyes of a Feng Shui expert, the result may be a little startling. It could be that there are hidden faults created by the actual energetic patterns of the buildings and their interiors.

If your business is struggling it may be in a black spot of stagnant energy in the midst of a busy area. The front door may be positioned in a way that fails to protect the building against noxious energies. Customers and clients may feel uncomfortable inside the premises. The staff may have a similar subtle feeling. Feng Shui masters sometimes speak of "angry energy" and if you have it circulating in your property, everyone will react against it, harming sales and creating disputes. Sometimes the arrangement of doorways can be harmful to many aspects of what goes on in a building. If there is a clear runway from the front door to the rear door (or an open arcade) money will tend to flow out from the building just as if there was a gaping hole in your pocket.

On the other hand, the application of Feng Shui principles by an experienced practitioner can pay handsome dividends, ensuring an invisible balance of energies, colors, shapes, and directions that create just the right working atmosphere – in which both customer and staff are happy to do business.

Locating the target

Your home is your base. In Feng Shui, the energy patterns that affect your home are some of the most important influences on your entire life. The first consideration is the exact location of your home. Most people's are located right beside or very near a road or street, and since thoroughfares are major conduits of energy the relationship of the road to your home is of prime importance. To understand how this works, think of your home as if it were a potential target. If the road is curved, as in the drawing on the right, the road is positioned like the bow of an archer opposite the two blue houses. This is the side of the curve that you should avoid. You can see how energy moving in either direction along the roadway (and that includes the traffic) can tend to skid off the curve and impact on the two blue houses. The blue houses are sitting targets; the yellow one is safe.

Curved energy flow
This energy flow (right) is rather like a river. If either end of the curve is higher than the other, the water flowing downward will normally stay confined between the banks. But if there is heavy rainfall or the river is swollen the first houses to be affected will be those directly in the line of the forward-moving water, or energy. Again, the blue houses will be in trouble.

66

Right-angled curve and U shape

The energy comes to a right-angled curve in the road (above). If is it moving slowly, it will turn the corner and bypass the blue house. If it is agitated or uncontrolled, it will miss the turning and carry straight on, hitting the blue house. The curve is like a band of warmth: the yellow house nicely embraced: the blue house excluded. If the house is located at the end of a complete U in the road (above right), the two powerful energy lines are catapulted on to the target of the blue house and form a point like the tip of a knife.

A speeding automobile

Using the target principle explained on this page, take a good look at this drawing (left). Imagine that the energy flow takes the form of a speeding automobile in the night. All three of these houses could be in danger, depending on which direction the car is heading. Think about and try to assess the most likely risks that each house will face.

67

Roundabouts and cul-de-sacs

Circular living

Some people live in circular settings, sometimes around a road interchange, sometimes in specially designed housing complexes. These may look attractive, but to the eye of the Feng Shui practitioner they both pose problems.

In the case of the roundabout, the energy spins, creating a vortex. Bands of energy shoot off at high velocity and bombard the houses. This subjects the households to constant disturbance. From the safety point of view, collisions and accidents, such as brake failures, can result in automobiles following the spinning energy lines and ploughing into houses on the margin.

Enclave living

A quiet dead-end street or a designer enclave like this may look like just the place for some peace and quiet. But imagine the energy entering the open end of the street and finding nowhere to go. It literally piles up like stagnant water at one end of a pond or like multiple vehicles ramming into each other on a blocked freeway. The families that live closest to the dead end will probably find comparable effects in their lives: a sense of having nowhere to go, or of having no future. It is unlikely that they will have a vibrant social life or that their businesses will thrive. The impact of the colliding and stagnating energy may also lead to disturbances in their family lives.

Three Fire buildings dominate these pages, each in a different cultural setting, each serving a different purpose, and yet all striking in their intensity and power.

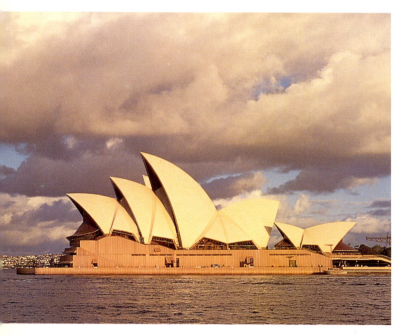

Fire shapes

The irregular triangles of the Sydney Opera House (above) lick the sky like flames. Seen from this angle, the whole structure has the quality of a craft with full sails: when the energy of the Wind and Water move together in certain directions, this ingenious structure draws that power to itself and to the city that surrounds it. Small wonder that Sydney will host the Olympics of the millennium!

Fire color

St. Basil's (left), with its world-famous domes, rises above the Kremlin in Moscow. It is a striking example of a Fire building – triangular in shape and predominantly red. It conveys tremendous power. If its energy acts as your mother, the protection it affords is immense. But if that energy is turned against you, you face a mighty enemy.

Fire structure

This pyramid at the Louvre in Paris (above) was designed by the Chinese architect responsible for the Bank of China in Hong Kong (p. 79). It is a superb Fire structure, drawing down intense energy from the heavens – and making this site a prodigious attraction for visitors. It is perfectly balanced with the Water structure of the Louvre.

The house on the hill

Perhaps you are thinking of moving from the city to the countryside. In the rolling contours of the landscape, where do you find a home that meets the basic Feng Shui requirements? You have already been provided in Part One with certain basic templates that you can use to assess a site.

If you use the model of The Five Animals (see pp. 38-9) when considering the house at the top of the hill (**1**), you will see that it has no tortoise, no dragon, and no tiger. So is it completely exposed and unsupported. Your ordinary common sense may tell you that this is a house that will be exposed to the elements and lashed periodically by the fury of nature.

The houses farther down the hill can use the natural terrain as a tortoise at their backs – if the doors of the houses are positioned so that the hill is at the rear. But that is not the only requirement. As you come down the hill, one house (**2**) is right in line with a sharp turn in the winding road. Using the principles described on pages 66-7, you can see that this house is a target – vulnerable to road accidents, torrential rains, and mudslides. Farther along is a house (**3**) in a far more suitable position, backed by the hill and on the safe side of the bend in the road.

Farther away is a mid-level house (**4**) in a very gently sloping dip that is shaped almost like a wok, the round Chinese frying vessel. This is a suitable contour in which to have a home, unlike the house at the far left of the drawing (**5**) which is sitting in an almost cup-like depression. That house is imprisoned in the hillside and the earth comes up in front of it, blocking its phoenix aspect.

You can use the principles shown in this very simplified sketch when looking at other homes. Is there a raised motorway that blocks the view from the front of the house? What lies at the back of the home? Do you get the feeling that the overall landscape around the area of the house is unbalanced, or does it conform to the model of The Five Animals?

5

The bridge

Go for an exhilarating walk across a bridge. Stand still in the middle, looking out over the expanse of water and the shoreline. Stroll back over the bridge and embrace in the moonlight. But, whatever you do, don't set up your home in a house built at either end!

The energy generated by bridges is tremendous. They attract people from far and wide and it is no wonder that artisans and hawkers have set out their stalls on these marvellous constructions from time immemorial. Not surprisingly it is in the very nature of a bridge to become a scene of raging battle in wartime.

The access points to a bridge are areas of conflict – with energy arriving in many directions, meeting the constant stream of energy pouring over the bridge and spilling outward. It is hard to imagine a less tranquil spot!

A bridge in conflict
This sketch, drawn from an old Chinese painting, shows the defence against pirates in Shangjin-Tielingguan.

Concentrations of energy

In many modern cities the traffic patterns around major bridges demonstrate the intense and conflicting movements and concentrations of energy at these points in the metropolis. Such bustling junctions are conducive to office use and to commercial and entertainment sites, rather than private homes.

Water, the difficult

In the eight trigrams of the I Ching, water is associated with difficulty. Its energies are deep and dark. It is sometimes said to convey the feeling of an abyss. It is a very powerful force: it absorbs and stores energy. Its behaviour is far from predictable. It cuts across other energetic forces just as it washes away the trail of an animal that plunges from the land into a stream.

Therefore the advice of a Feng Shui practitioner is always to be very careful about locations that involve water. To begin with, do not live in a house that has a body of water at its back. The effect of the water energy can be disturbing in a number of ways, producing health problems and sexual disorders, and it can affect the dwelling by seeping into the foundations and causing it to sink.

Using the template of The Five Animals (see pp. 38-9) you can immediately understand the advice against water at the back. The place of maximum solidity should be toward the rear of the house. Any body of water to the rear weakens that all-important quality of strength and support.

Advice on water
The Feng Shui advice on water is as true in the urban environment as it is in the countryside (below). The back gardens of homes may adjoin public parks, with streams or pools, or may open on to canals. The advice is the same: the only advisable place for a body of water is to the front of your dwelling.

Facing a stream
The house on the near side of the stream (above) is well positioned. But if the water were stagnant (as in a disused canal) or too close to the front of the house, its energy would not bode well for the home (see pp. 52-3).

The house on the far side of the stream is not in a safe position. The house is a target for the "bow" of the stream as it flows past. It has no protection against sudden overflow and is excluded from the protective circulation from which the house on the opposite side benefits.

Energy convergence

The Taj Mahal (above) is one of the world's greatest pieces of architectural poetry. The design is beautifully balanced and the arrangement of the central building and its candle-like towers are perfectly suited to a tomb. However, the long reflecting pond and the two pathways create a powerful line of energy converging on the very heart of the main building. To the Feng Shui expert this would affect the health and stability of the ruler who built it, as well as his long-term political power – which did indeed begin to dwindle after the Taj was completed.

Silent power

The obelisk of the Washington Monument (left) towers above the central institutions of the United States. Its spear-like power emanates in all directions, affecting the Capitol building of the Congress, the Supreme Court, and the White House. Like a mighty sword raised in the air, it is a constant, silent presence: those who live and work within its reach will often find themselves subject to internal disturbance and their ability to make decisions blocked.

Angular energy

Like the polished blade of a meat cleaver, the new Bank of China building (above) rises above the Hong Kong skyline. All those in offices nearby sought the advice of Feng Shui experts for protection against the angular energy of this structure. It is a spectacular expression of power – perfectly positioned with the mountains to the rear and the harbour to the front – giving the impression of a rocket ready for lift off.

Certain places, certain effects

The location of your home is decisive in creating a harmonious life. The energy that affects your home may come from inconceivably distant places within our galaxy or elsewhere in the universe. Ordinarily this is not easy to ascertain and the special training of a Feng Shui expert is required. But it is possible to work with this principle in making your own assessment of possible locations for your home. For example, instead of simply wondering if you are moving into a "nice neighbourhood" or thinking solely about the convenience to transportation or local food shops, you can try to sense the broader feel of the locality and the quality of its energy. Individuals have varying sensitivities to this, but it is by no means rare.

You can use the basic information in this book as a guide. What are the contours of the land and the configuration of the roads – is the house in one of the positions you are warned against on pages 66-9? Where is the nearest open body of water, such as a pond, public swimming pool, or reservoir? Is it toward the back of the house or far in front? What is there in the nearby environment that you think could disturb the tranquillity of your home and particularly affect peaceful sleep?

You should also consider the human environment. A Feng Shui expert would never recommend that you occupy a home that is opposite or next door to places that regularly have a disturbed atmosphere or are associated with trouble, crime, or violent individuals. You probably wouldn't want to live there in any case, but the Feng Shui advice is to avoid homes opposite or adjacent to bars, brothels, and police stations. You should also avoid living opposite or next to buildings with the shape associated with the Fire element (see pp. 32-7).

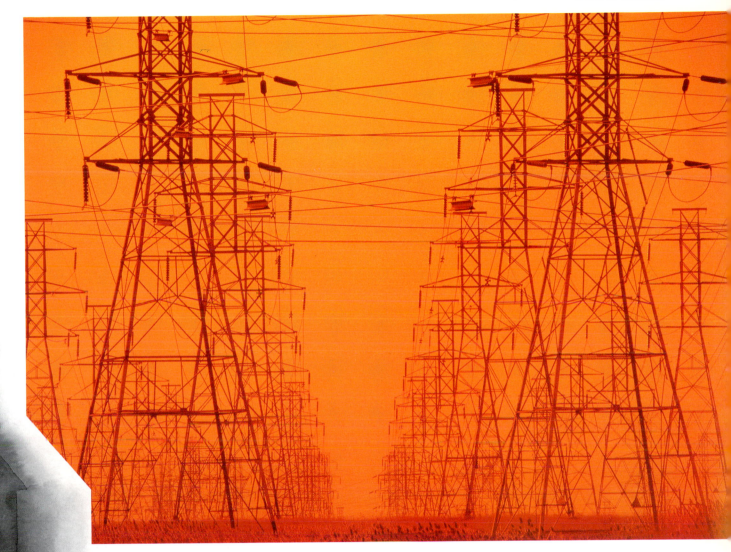

Disturbing influences

A streetlamp outside your home sets up an energy field that disturbs the space in front of your dwelling (left). This is easily understandable at night when the glare of the lamp is steadily beaming down. But, to the Feng Shui expert, the lamp post and its constant electrical field are disturbing influences throughout the day and night. Living under power lines (above) takes this problem to the extreme. It should be avoided at all costs as recent health studies on people suffering from leukemia and other cancers in such locations have shown.

Supports and pressures

Exerting pressures

Buildings exert different pressures on each other. A taller building (below left) plays the role of the tortoise in The Five Animals, giving weight, support, and protection to the one in front.

A child between two bullies

The little apartment building in the middle of these two tall buildings (right) is like a small child between two bullies. The taller structures support the sides of the little one, but their main effect is literally to suck energy away from it and to exert converging downward pressure.

High-pressure energy
Any home which is directly opposite a small gap between two buildings, whether they are tall like this (left), or little semi-detached houses, will be exposed to a constant stream of high pressure energy, said in Feng Shui to act on that home like a chopping knife.

Support on one side
The short building behind the tall one (above) has support on one side, but none on the other side. The arrangement is unbalanced: its dragon side is empty and its tiger side is far too dominant. A Feng Shui expert would advise you not to move in to the smaller building: there may be a risk of violence as a result of the powerful force on the tiger side.

Supportive but oppressive
If a building at the rear is clearly taller than the one in front, it is regarded as supportive, like the tortoise. But if it is just tall enough to peep over the top of the building in front, it is said to be like a person peering over your shoulder and its effect is oppressive. This building also suffers from being exposed to the knife-like pressure from the sharp corner of the office block opposite.

Mid-town Feng Shui

You live in the middle of a bustling city. You are
on the seventh floor of a nine-floor building.
Immediately behind your building rises a 16-floor
apartment block. To your left is another building,
just slightly taller that the one you live in. To the
right is a low arcade with small shops. There is a
wide street in front of your apartment building and
the town houses on the other side of the street are
set back from the pavement with a large forecourt.
There may be something about your own particular
apartment that you don't like, but you feel some
sense of attachment to the overall location itself.
It's no surprise: it conforms exactly to the prime
requirements of the model of the cave and the river
(strong support at the back and open space in
front). It also conforms exactly to the model of The
Five Animals: the solid tortoise in the rear, a rising
dragon on the left, a lower, active tiger on the
right, and space for your phoenix to fly ahead
in front.

Shapes and sightlines

The relationship of shapes to The Five Energies was explained in Part One (see pp. 36-7). The energetic qualities of shapes can have a marked effect on the lives of the people who live and work inside them. For example, your experience of sitting in a round room is very different to the feeling you have when seated in a square room. Similarly, you react to a room with a high curved ceiling in one way and in another way to a room with a sloping roof. The effect of shapes – not only on your feelings but on the general direction of your life – is part of the storehouse of Feng Shui wisdom. One example of this effect is connected with roofs (see below). But the shape of a building or a plot of land has significance as well. The contours affect the relationship of the enclosed space with the energy of the space that surrounds it. Some shapes attract energy to certain points in the structure, others repel it. Using this principle, it is possible to determine the most suitable points to locate yourself within the space. The incoming energy may be helpful or harmful to you – this depends on many factors; but the general principle in Feng Shui is that it is better to avoid those areas where energy is too concentrated lest you be subjected to the sustained impact of negative influences.

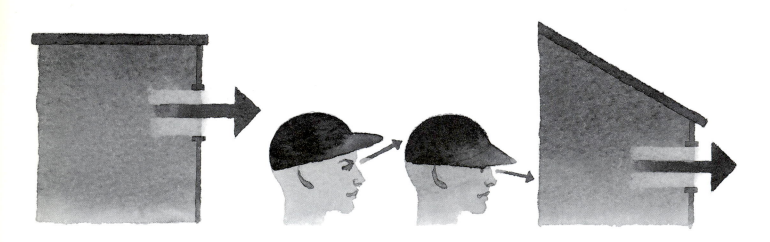

A clear sightline
A house needs a clear sightline, just as a person needs to be able to see straight ahead without obstruction. A level roof corresponds to a person whose cap is straight. Having a sloping roof over your head is like having the visor of your cap pulled down over your eyes. In Feng Shui, the family that lives in a house with a sloping roof will never advance, and a nation whose people live under such roofs will become inward-looking and stagnant.

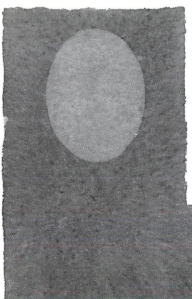

An L-shaped house

Energy converges on a L-shaped house (left). If the front door is there, accidents will happen and many other things will go wrong. If you are looking at flats in a block shaped like this, your best bet is to choose one at either of the ends, shown in a lighter tone, far away from the converging arrows.

Concave and convex curves

A curved surface that is concave (left) acts like a receiver. It draws energy toward itself. If you were to build a house on land with this shape, the safest locations would be at the two ends, with the entrance facing in toward the middle. An outward, convex curve (above) deflects the energy: even those beams that strike the middle fail to penetrate. Any location inside such a space is relatively protected.

Your front door

The front of your home is like your face. Your front door is your mouth. You should give great care to this vital element of your home. There are two important points on which you would be advised if you consulted a Feng Shui expert. The first concerns the access route to your front door. Try to make sure that any path, stairway, or corridor leading directly up to your front door does not resemble a straight arrow, pole, or the barrel of a gun. Straight lines leading to the door are to be avoided if at all possible. (If you are looking at apartments to rent, pay attention to the arrangement of the corridors in the building, as if you were studying the energy movements on the roads shown on pp. 66-7.) There is a second important question to ask: is there more than one front entrance to the house? In Feng Shui, homes with two front doors in use are held to be like people with two mouths: unreliable, confused, and argumentative! A harmonious home has only one front door. If you are designing a domestic entrance for people with disabilities, the same principle applies: one door for the whole family.

A protected front door
The pond (right) is positioned on the outside of the curved approach to the house. The arrangement protects the front door from direct, angular energy "attacks". Note that the house is on the safe side of the curving road in front.

A combination of doors
A revolving door flanked by two ordinary doorways (above) is a common sight at the entrance to hotels, department stores, and theatres. This is fine for public buildings and other places through which people pass in transit. It would be most inappropriate – and unlikely – for a private dwelling.

"One face, one mouth"
The principle of "one face, one mouth" applies to access routes to main entrances (right). It is common to see double approaches or curving stairways swirling up from different angles to public buildings. To the Feng Shui expert, this is the equivalent of having two tongues – a sure recipe for perpetual argument and discord among all who work inside.

The power of rock

Everything in nature expresses its own energetic force. Recognizing this is essential to creating a living environment in which Yin and Yang are balanced. Rock is an extremely powerful form of energy; it is the Metal of The Five Energies. One never knows exactly how Metal energy will behave, and the uneven and angular formation of most rock means that it often has a disruptive influence on the circulation of other energies in the immediate area. For this reason, Feng Shui experts strongly advise against placing rocks or rock gardens at the entrance to your home. If you recall the basic features of The Five Animal template, the area in front of your dwelling should be open, smooth, and unobstructed.

Rocks in front
Look at the front of this house (right): imagine it is a face. You can then see how the "mouth" is being blocked up by the ascending pile of rocks. It may look very attractive from one point of view, but to the eyes of the trained Feng Shui practitioner, the rock garden should be replaced with smooth lawn.

A disrupted phoenix
Even the curved path leading up to the front door (left) cannot solve the funda-mental problem caused by the large rock that disrupts the phoenix aspect of this house.

A "good Feng Shui" entrance
The position of this rock birdbath (above) is fortuitous. The path that curves around it meets to become a single path leading to the front door. Having some water like this, in the reasonably open front space, is "good Feng Shui".

A cluttered entrance
An unobstructed front door is important to the health of your home. Don't clut-ter up your entrance. Here (left) there is a pile of logs, but stones or equipment would create a similar problem.

91

Trees and creepers

The Chinese have always recognized the great power of trees. They are among the greatest manifestations of the transforming power of nature. But, as with all things, it is our Yin and Yang relationship with them that determines the effect that they will have. For this reason, the location of trees, bushes, and creepers around the home should be carefully considered. Shrubbery should not be treated as merely decorative: as the illustration on these pages shows, each of these charming little homes has a problem.

1. *The straight path leading up to the front door, provides an unobstructed route for the impact of potentially harmful energy. The large tree is too close to the front, disrupting the smooth flow of energy in the all-important open space. The large trees at the rear are too close: they keep too much of the house in shade and their roots may affect the foundations.*

2. *The curved path is a definite improvement over the straight path of the neighbours, but the two bushes outside the front door are reminiscent of the candles that burn on either side of memorials to the dead. One bush on its own or two bushes, one higher and one lower, would not create this problem.*

3. *This little house has three problems with its entrance. You can spot the trouble with the pathway. As long as the bushes at the far end of the path remain relatively low, there is no problem; but if they are allowed to rise up, then the sense of a tomb will be created. The walls of your house are like your skin: creepers affect the ability of the building material to breathe and the inhabitants often develop skin problems themselves.*

4. If this last house had a neighbor on its left side (or close by), or a large tree reasonably near to it on that side, it would be far more suitable. As it stands its dragon side is completely open. Also the bush growing against the wall, like the creeper next door, will affect the "skin" of the house.

Your bedroom – privacy and peace

Most of us spend at least one-third of our lives in our bedrooms. Most of that time we are asleep. This part of our lives is extremely important to us. We need to sleep well – deep, refreshing sleep. We need to dream – clear, regenerative dreams.

For many people, the bedroom is also one of the places of greatest intimacy in our lives. We are alone with ourselves, or with our partners. It is one of the rooms in which we are most frequently naked, without adornment of any kind. It is a place of private conversation, whispers, and pillow talk. And when we are asleep, we are often at our most vulnerable.

Our bedroom serves not only as a place of privacy, it is also a refuge. It is often here that we come for protection, for security, and peace. We can "sleep" on our problems. We can curl up, turning away from the stress of the daytime – switching off the conscious activities of the brain and allowing the unconscious mind free rein.

If these precious hours of sleep and recuperation are disturbed, we all know the dreadful price we pay. If the bedroom is not a place of harmonious living between husband and wife, between partners, or between children or roommates, the consequences for our home lives can be devastating – and how often we have seen that devastation exported emotionally into the rest of our lives!

As you have already seen, the physical layout of any room can either enhance or endanger the essential qualities that you should have there. This is just as true of the bedroom.

Which room is more peaceful?
In addition to the arrangement of your bedroom furniture, all the other aspects of the room must be taken into account – the wall colors, the lighting, the floor covering, decorations, ornaments, and plants. If you look at these two pictures of actual bedrooms, you get an immediate sense of which one is more peaceful and more conducive to the essential qualities you need in this most important room in your house.

The position of your bedroom

The location of the bedroom in your home is important. If you are buying or renting a new place to live, you should pay careful attention to the internal relationship between the bedroom and the rest of the space. Since the energies from the rest of the home enter the bedroom principally through the bedroom door, it is essential that you are particularly careful about the areas of the home on to which the door opens.

This may not seem all that important to you and, anyway, the options you have may be limited.

But remember that you will likely be spending such a great deal of your time in your bedroom and that you will be profoundly affected by the subtle influences of the energies that enter and circulate in that room.

You want to have a bedroom that is as safe as possible, where your privacy is ensured, where the risk of intruders is minimal, and where the risk of accident is reduced. Remember that these qualities are all the more important to you when it is dark and you are asleep.

Work area

Solid bookcase

Sleeping area

Moveable
screen

Solving open-plan problems
You may find that there is no door on the bedroom, or that the layout of the whole home is open-plan. This may expose you, while sleeping, to many unsuitable influences and you may find that you lack a secure, quiet place of repose. In the world of Feng Shui you should try to have a separate bedroom with a door. If this is not possible, then you should try to set up your living space so that the sleeping area is clearly defined and protected at night by a barrier such as a bookcase or a screen.

The alignment of your bedroom door

You should pay particular attention to the relationship of your bedroom door to other doors or openings in your home. Energies can easily flow from one room to another if there is a direct line of movement through the door-ways. In some homes the entrance to the bedroom is directly in line with the front door. This is a particularly insecure arrangement. Remember, the bedroom should be one of the most interior, private places in your home. In other homes you sometimes find the entrance to the bedroom is directly in line with the bathroom or the kitchen. These arrangements are unsuitable, mainly because they make the bedroom vulnerable to odors, fumes, and noxious energies.

97

The bedroom animals

People who have heard a little about Feng Shui often ask: "How should I arrange my bedroom". And if you listen to the contradictory advice they get, you might easily get very confused. It is very likely that if you were to invite a Feng Shui expert to help you arrange your bedroom you might be asked questions about your date of birth and so on – because of the nine aspects of Feng Shui explained in Part One of this book. Nevertheless, even without such expert advice, there are a few common, basic principles that you can use.

You have already seen how you could use The Five Animals template (see pp. 38-9) to help assess the suitability of a location for your home. Here you see how it applies to your bedroom. You are always the snake at the center.

The position of your bed is the most important consideration. Whether you are aware of it or not, you have a particular need for security when your consciousness is in the resting phase. If your bed is in an unsuitable position, your nervous system remains on constant alert. Pay attention to your tortoise side – in other words the area directly behind your head. Make sure it is solid.

Next in importance is the area in front of you: your phoenix aspect. Leave as much room as you can at the foot of your bed.

To the left side of your bed is the dragon side – the ideal position for tall items such as a clothes cupboard or shelving. Your right side, the tiger side, is best for low furniture, such as a bedside table or storage chest.

Beds and doors

The picture below speaks for itself. No door, no privacy. You could almost say "no door, no room". It's something you can live with in a hotel suite for a few nights, but this arrangement does not meet the requirements of a place into which you can retire securely at night. Your inner being will remain on the alert.

The other six sketches advise you on where to place your bed – and where not to put it – in relation to the door of your bedroom. Don't put it on the wall beside the door where you cannot see who is entering the room until they are already inside (**1**). Don't put it in the middle of the room facing the door; this is too exposed (**2**). Don't put it directly opposite the door where it is directly in line with the incoming energy (**3** and **4**).

The last two positions (**5** and **6**) are suitable since they are out of the line of incoming energy, but still enable you to keep the door conveniently in sight.

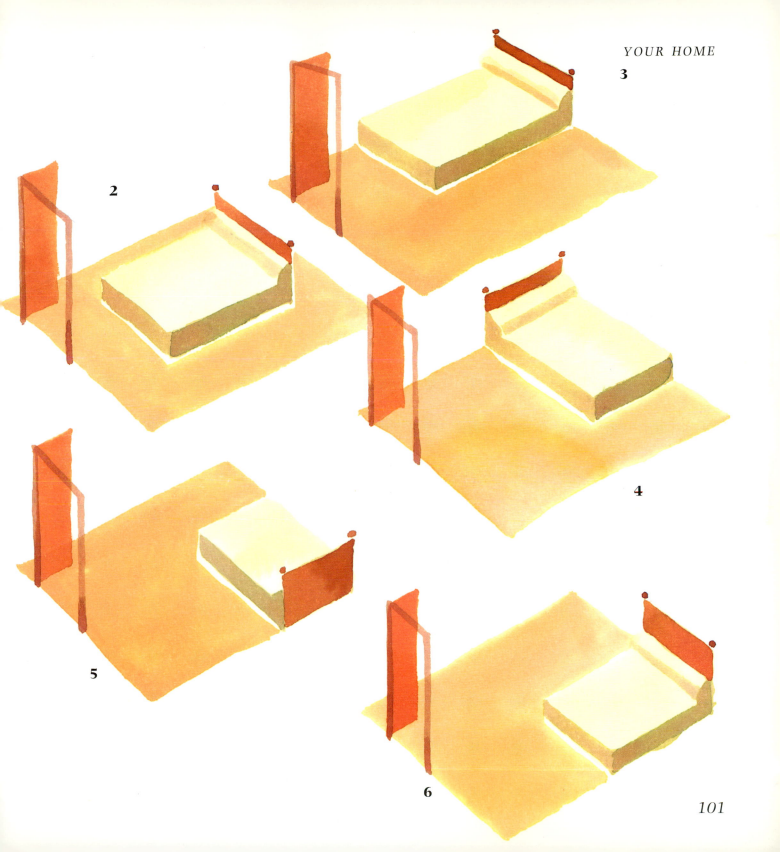

3

2

4

5

6

Windows and beds

One of the main factors that determines how energy circulates in your bedroom is the alignment of the windows and the door (see pp. 44-5). It is very important, therefore, to take the relative positions of the windows and door into account in deciding where to place your bed. You want to avoid sleeping in the equivalent of an "energy draft" and, at the same time, you don't want to be in too stagnant an area of the room. Pulling the curtains or blinds over the windows when you are using your bed is a simple solution if the location of the windows is a problem.

Constant current
As energy enters the room (above), it travels over to the windows and therefore creates a constant current over the bed.

Energy passes through
The energy enters through the door (above) and will pass straight out the other side through the floor-to-ceiling window. The bed is in a poor position in relation to the door (see pp. 100-1).

Bed in a good location
The bed is not next to the windows (right), so it is less affected by energy currents passing through them.

Under a window
The head of the bed is directly under a window (left). If the blind is left open, then the tortoise side is unsupported. If the blind is pulled down, then the window is covered and this becomes a suitable position for the bed.

A good position
The bed (above) has been placed in the most sensible position in relation to the windows on the two walls and the door.

What are the problems here?
You now have enough information at your disposal (see also pp. 46-7) to be able to determine the problems associated with the position of this bed (left). You should take into account the relationship to the door, to the overhead beam, and the overhead window.

103

Mirror power

A common mistake is to think of a mirror as an inert object, a useful tool, like a screwdriver. But mirrors are constantly at work, not only when we pass them and look at them. They intensify the image of anything that they reflect. Think about what happens when you shine an electric torch or flashlight into a mirror at night. The light that bounces back to you is far more blinding that the naked beam of the small bulb.

So the first rule is never place a mirror directly opposite the door of your bedroom (**1**). It will bounce the incoming energy straight back at the door, where it will set up permanent disturbance patterns at the entrance to your bedroom and prevent smooth circulation inside the room.

High-intensity bounce-back

*Mirrors positioned opposite windows will have the same bounce-back effect as those opposite doors, leading to a constant, narrow band of disturbance between the window and the mirror (**2**). A mirror positioned so that you can see the bed from the door will have the same effect as if the door were directly opposite the bed, but remember that the energy bounced off the mirror will be of higher intensity (**3**).*

Perpetual disturbance

*Avoid placing a mirror opposite your bed. Remember that it acts as a constant energy reflector and will be sending that stream of intensified power into the space over and around your bed, day and night. It will be a perpetual cause of disturbance while you sleep (**4** and **5**). Ideally, you should place your mirror on the inside of a cupboard door (**6**). If you are staying in a strange room, use a scarf to cover an unwanted mirror.*

105

Headaches and disturbances

Many people wake up from a night's sleep and feel awful. Often they complain about having a headache, or they may feel as if they had a headache during the night. They can't put their finger on it, but they know that they have had a disturbed night's sleep.

There may be many, many reasons for this – it is not all down to the location of their home or the arrangement of rooms and furniture. So simply rearranging things will not necessarily solve the problem. On the other hand, you can have a look around your bedroom to see if there are any possible reasons that could contribute to poor sleep. For example, some storage arrangements can cause real problems from the Feng Shui perspective.

Storage drawers
Under-the-bed storage drawers are convenient, and a good solution. These should be used for utility goods such as bedding, towels, and blankets. A low storage chest at the foot of your bed is fine, too.

Built-in storage
All-in-one storage arrangements for the bedroom (right) often provide behind-the-bed storage, complete with wall mirror. The mirror is unsuitable (see pp. 104-5) and although the head of the bed is against something solid, you should try to keep the immediate area behind you free of objects and ornaments. To be tranquil, the space should be clear. Incidentally, have you spotted the problem of the window with no curtains opposite the side of the bed (see pp. 102-3)?

Enclosed head space

If you were to look straight down into this room (above) so that you had a bird's eye view, you would be unable to see the heads of the sleeping occupants, because the entire head area of the bed is enclosed in the storage cupboard area. While it is good to have the solidity on the "tortoise side", the overhanging cupboards create a constant downward pressure, just like an overhead beam (see pp. 46-7).

Solving the overhang problem

If you have overhanging bookshelves (right), one solution, apart from moving your bed, is to use the whole wall for shelving and finish it off part way down with a large storage area with sliding doors. This would avoid the problem of putting your head under the shelves.

Your bedroom style

Getting the right mix of features and materials in your bedroom is important. In deciding how to arrange any room, how to decorate it, and what to put in it, the main purpose of the room is the most important consideration.

The overall style of your bedroom, therefore, needs to reflect the importance of this area as one in which your whole being (body and mind) comes for repose. This is an indispensable aspect of the perpetual process of Yin and Yang (see pp. 18-23), and if you do not respect it, an essential aspect of the balance of your life will go out of kilter.

Tombstone headboard
It doesn't take much imagination to see that the headboard of this bed (above) resembles a tombstone. Such similarities would immediately strike the eye of the Feng Shui expert and you would be advised to select a different style.

Plants in the bedroom
During the day, plants take in carbon dioxide and produce oxygen. So plants and flowers around a sickbed (left) make sense in the daytime. But at night the pattern of gas exchange is reversed and they compete with us for oxygen. Don't fill your bedroom with plants and, if you're ill, remove the gifts of greenery overnight.

Unpredictable energy

From the Feng Shui point of view, bed frames should be made of warm materials, not metal (below) which is cold and has unpredictable energetic qualities. Nor is the bedroom a religious sanctuary, so according to Feng Shui principles it should not be used as a place of worship. If you have nowhere else to put items of religious significance, the best arrangement is to keep them in a little cabinet that you can keep closed.

High-energy patterns

Not everyone would want to decorate their bedroom like this (above) and a Feng Shui practitioner would certainly advise against it! You can imagine the high-speed, topsy-turvy energy patterns that bounce around a room with wall-to-wall and full-ceiling mirrors! And the skins of dead animals, whether of tigers or sheep or any other creature, definitely have no place in a room of harmony.

Lights and colors

Light is energy in one of its most obvious forms. What we perceive as color is, of course, light as well. Its power is incalculable, yet most of us take it almost for granted. You need only reflect on the mystery of the dawn and the slow pageant of the sunset to understand how completely light and color transform the entire world, our perceptions of it, and our own lives. In the same way, light and color in our homes are an integral part of the quality of life we have there – and a major factor in influencing the interplay of Yin and Yang. Change the colors of the walls or doors, put in new lights and your home is changed. So the Feng Shui practitioner takes lighting very seriously indeed, and also warns against inappropriate lights and colors.

Overhead lighting
An overhead lights sends a powerful shower of energy streaming down over the bed. Feng Shui experts would advise you to avoid this arrangement, especially if the light is positioned over the head of the bed. Even when the light is switched off, the electrical circuitry is in place, subtly affecting the energy movements in the area and, most particularly, underneath.

Downlighting
Positioning two lights over the bed so that they shine down over the heads of the people using it may be convenient for reading, but from the Feng Shui point of view it is regarded as potentially harmful for health. Reading lights should be placed beside the bed.

Soft tones

These are ideal for your bedroom – warm pink tints and pale peach shades. You find these toward the reddish end of the spectrum and also in the off-white tints such as eggshell, magnolia, beige, and light tan. Very pale purples, light magentas, and violets are also suitable in the bedroom as long as they create a soft, relaxing effect. Strong reds, wine colors, and orange tones are too overpowering and not suitable for indoor, domestic use.

Yellow and strong earth colors

These work very well in the kitchen and are a perfect correspondence in The Five Energy system, but are not appropriate for use in your bedroom, living room, or bathroom.

The blue end of the spectrum

This is not recommended for use as a room color in Feng Shui. Dark blues, the colors of deep water, are particularly avoided. The use of very light blues in the living room is sometimes acceptable, but the cumulative effect tends to make people withdrawn and introspective.

Light greens

These are cool colors, relaxing and easy on the eyes. You can use them in your bedroom and also in your sitting room and bathroom. Dark green tones, however, are too heavy and are not generally recommended for the home.

Pure, brilliant white

This is not recommended for domestic walls, but cream colors, warm off-white tints, and beige tones are suitable in almost any room. The warmer tints are best suited to your bedroom, living room, and kitchen. Cooler shades may be used in your bathroom and other utility rooms.

This is very general advice and should not be taken as a set of fixed rules. Indeed, if you engage a Feng Shui expert to assist you in arranging your home, you may be given very different instructions – follow that specialist advice, since it will be adapted to your particular circumstances and the conditions prevailing at that time.

Your living room: taking your seat

When you arrange your living room, the key aspect to consider is the position of the main sitting area. In the Feng Shui tradition this is the place where the head or heads of the household normally sit when using the room. In many homes the sofa or settee is placed here or it could be the position for your favourite chair. In the drawings on this page the sofa is used to mark this spot. A common mistake is to leave too much space between the sofa and the wall, thus leaving you vulnerable from the rear (**1** and **4**). If the door opens behind you – or if there is a window right behind you – this problem is made all the worse (**1** and **2**). Similarly, it is not wise to place the sofa so that you are seated with the door to one side (**2** and **5**). Positioning the sofa so that it is directly opposite the door should be avoided, since you will be exposed to a stream of energy entering the room which is directed at you like a beam (**3**).

1

The best location
In this room, the best position for the sofa is toward the corner away from the both the door and the window (right). Here you can sit comfortably with your back to the wall, without disturbance from the doorway, and command the entire room. The sofa need not be touching both walls of the corner, as long as the back of the sofa is against one of the walls. For example, there could be a small side table in the corner between one wall and the arm of the sofa.

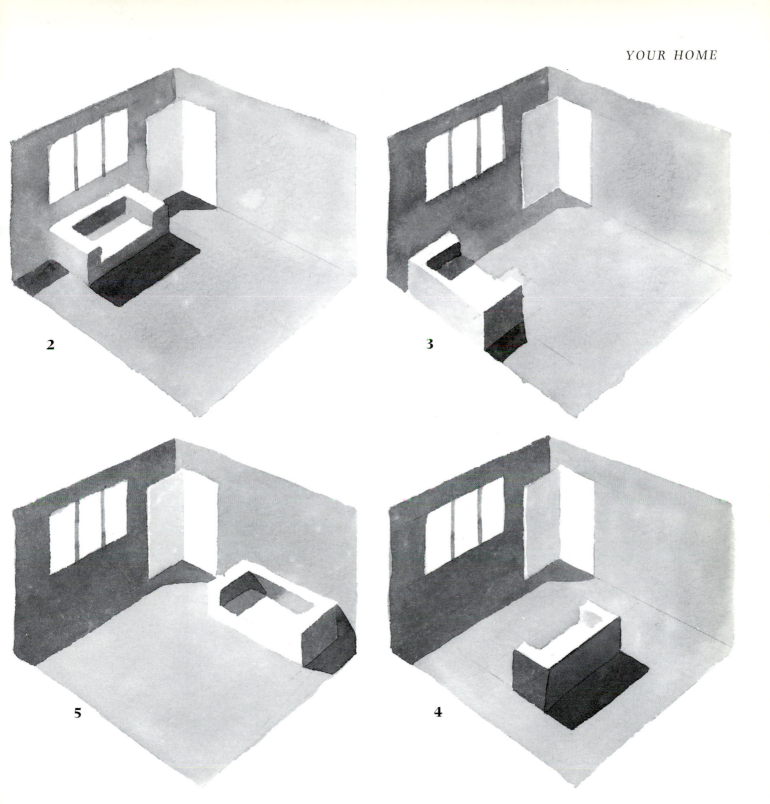

Feng Shui in the open

Supposing you don't have a separate living room but live in an apartment or studio flat where you must accommodate a number of functions in a relatively open space. You can still apply the basic Feng Shui principles, as the tenants of this one-bedroom apartment have done. The kitchen (lower far right) is kept a bit more separate by using folding doors on the two walk-through spaces; the eating area is within easy access, but a little apart from the main sitting area (center right). A large decorative screen is used to create a "wall" behind the sofa area so that its space is defined and protected. The television (top) is positioned in front of the sitting area, but is in a cabinet so that the windows behind it do not prevent daytime viewing. The little office area (center) has been carefully arranged so that one bookcase provides a back wall behind the desk chair and the other is sufficiently far forward that there is still some space beyond the desk.

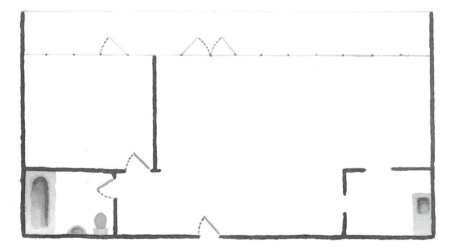

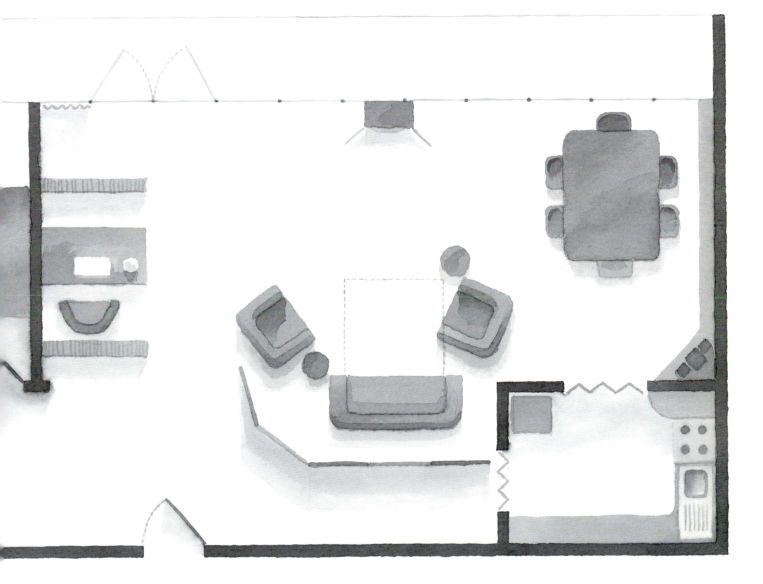

Living in space

In order to arrange your living room in the best possible way, you should keep in mind the fact that you are living in space. As you saw in Part One (pp. 16-17), the apparently solid objects that surround you are fields of energy and you also need to be sensitive to what is happening in the space between them. On the ground floor of this home (above), energy enters through the front door (lower right corner) and, if the French doors in the living room are open, will pass straight out. Otherwise the energy circulates through the living room and around the other connecting rooms. The curtains are closed on the far walls (top), hence the smooth lines of energy movement there. By reflecting on such movements, you can consider where best to situate yourself – and where to avoid.

Knocked-through living area

Apply your understanding of energy movement to this common floor plan (above). The original wall separating two rooms has been knocked down to create a large living area. The dining table has been placed in the front of the room, near windows facing the street. The rear half of the room is used as the sitting room. If the two doors and various windows are open, consider how the energy might move and ask yourself: "Why would a Feng Shui expert advise me to place the sofa in the corner, where it is now, rather than in the center of the room opposite the fireplace?" (see pp. 112-13)

Corner compression

If you want to organize your living room furniture on diagonal lines, you need to think about the way energy behaves in corners. The two walls act like pincers, creating a sense of compression in the corner. In this room (above), the problem has been solved by having a corner cupboard behind the sofa – the main sitting area. The chairs in the other corners should be used for visitors.

Disturbing pressures

Avoid sitting for long periods under overhead beams or lights (above). The energetic pressures they create can be very disturbing – and the impact on the psyche is even greater if you are exposed to them for long periods in an undefended position.

Life styles

When you put something in your home, you are bringing that energy into your life. When you paint your walls or put up wall paper, the energy of those colors and materials changes your home. When you buy a rug for the floor, you are adding a new pattern of energy to your environment. Here are two very different décors: the choice between them is not exactly the same as a choice between two photographs, because these are snapshots of vibrant environments that will affect every individual who moves inside them. The choice in décor is therefore not merely a question of what you like at any particular moment, but what effect these designs will have upon your life.

Different décors

The sharp, angular design of the room containing challenging artwork and metallic-frame furniture is very cold. It is neither relaxing nor inviting. In this room you will be constantly on the alert and perpetually nervous. It looks striking, but it is a place of exhaustion. The dark, ornate living room is also oppressive, but in a different way. The mirrors create chaotic energy patterns, to which the wallpaper contributes. The weapons add to the latent violence. It can be disturbing to be told these things by a Feng Shui expert, but they are warnings that you are surrounded by disturbance. Feng Shui advice is never meant as personal criticism!

Kitchen positions

Food is treated with great care in Chinese culture. It is sometimes referred to as a form of "post-natal Chi" – meaning that once we are born, food supplies us with the vital energy of the universe. How food is prepared and where it is prepared is all part of the process of sustaining our life force. If that process is disturbed, the energy of the food will be affected and the disturbance transmitted to all those who eat it.

As with the other rooms of the house, therefore, the position of your kitchen is extremely important. The kitchen entrance should not be directly opposite your front door (right), in order to protect it from any incoming harmful energies. The heat of cooking and the materials, such as grease, that it releases into the atmosphere should not be allowed to penetrate the rest of your home. So make sure that your kitchen doesn't open on to your living room or bedroom (below); if it does, keep the doors closed whenever cooking is in progress.

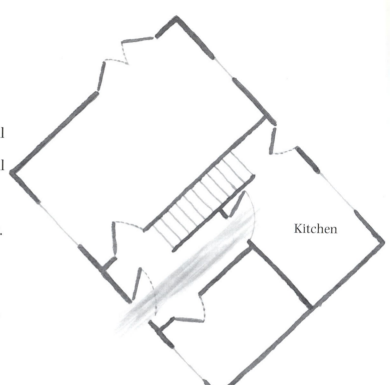

Kitchen

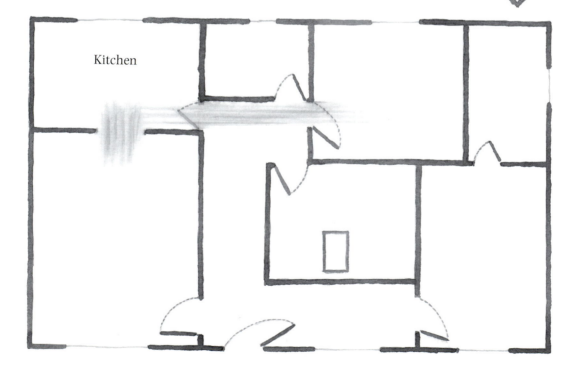

Kitchen

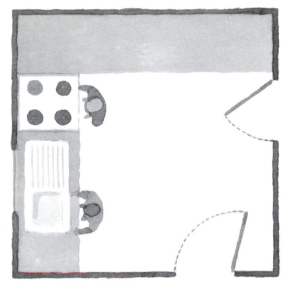

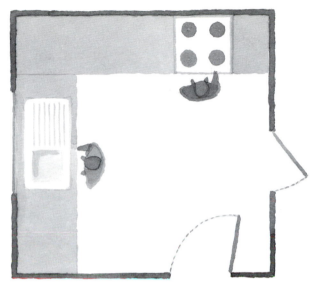

Uneasy cooking

When you stand at the oven/stove the door is directly behind you. If it is open, your tortoise side is unprotected, which contributes to a sense of unease when you should be calm.

Exposed back

Here, too, your back is in a direct line to an open door, whether you are at the oven/stove or sink. Neither position is free from tension. The only thing you can do is close the door.

Stove by a window

The oven/stove is directly in front of the window. In Feng Shui this is a problem because the oven/stove is the modern hearth of the home and is a significant force. Its tortoise side should be protected and hence its back should be not be against a window.

A good layout

This is a good layout for your kitchen. It has none of the problems associated with the other plans on this page. If your kitchen is arranged appropriately, your food, your health, and your family will prosper.

121

Kitchen styles

Two families have very different tastes when it comes to decorating their kitchens. Both are determined to have all the latest conveniences and to be right up-to-date with interior design trends. The problem is that there are just so many design possibilities – even a very traditional or rustic kitchen can now be in great demand. After a lot of discussion, each family settles for a distinctive approach – one chooses a "high-tech" look, the other goes for a "country kitchen".

Examined from the point of view of Feng Shui, the fashionable appearances are not all that important. What is taken into account in assessing the energy of the room are the structural aspects, the arrangement of key kitchen furniture, and the colors, textures, and shapes.

In the shiny smooth kitchen (near right), the walls are bright white and the kitchen units are a mix of brilliant white surfaces and chrome fittings. The extractor over the hob is chrome, too. By contrast, the kitchen table and the stools are high-gloss ebony. The flooring is grey carpet tiles with black striping. If you refer to the color chart on page 111, you will see that this color scheme is far too cold for a harmonious kitchen and does not correspond to the color associations of The Five Energies system (see pp. 32-5).

Having an extractor over the oven/stove is highly recommended, but in this case the polished chrome brings a powerful column of Metal energy into the kitchen, which is a room of Earth energy.

In the cycles of the Five Energies (see pp. 34-5) if Metal energy is too strong, it represses Wood energy, the parent of Earth. If Wood is repressed, then the Earth energy becomes sluggish. This is a good example of how you can use the scheme of the Five Energies to analyze the effect of materials and objects on each other – and on you.

Peasant-style kitchen

This kitchen (above) has certain attractive features, but presents several problems from the Feng Shui point of view. The central area, the snake, is completely obstructed by the large table. There is no extractor over the oven/stove so the excess energies of cooking circulate through the entire kitchen. The exposed knives hanging from the table cut the atmosphere and are dangerous. The floor tiling is potentially slippery (cork tiling is preferable) – and overhead the energy patterns of the beams rain down like hammers (see pp. 46-7)

Bathroom/toilet: using the human model

The functions of releasing and eliminating waste material from the body are essential life processes. Like the other vital functions of a human being they have particular organs and mechanisms. Following this same principle, the location of the bathroom/toilet in your home is just as important as that of any of the other rooms and has a bearing on your living arrangements. In this way, your home can be understood as a model of the human body and its functions – and arranged accordingly.

In some countries, the bathroom/toilet is in a separate room to the bath; in other countries all such facilities are put together in the same room. For the purposes of Feng Shui, both are considered to have broadly the same purpose and so in this book they are examined as one unit.

Facing the front door
The bathroom/toilet should not face the door (above) due to energy movement problems (see pp. 96-7).

Next to the kitchen
The bathroom/toilet should not be next to the kitchen. (left) If you have no choice, be sure to keep the door closed at all times. In many countries this layout is illegal for reasons of hygiene. Such prohibition in law is in line with good Feng Shui practice.

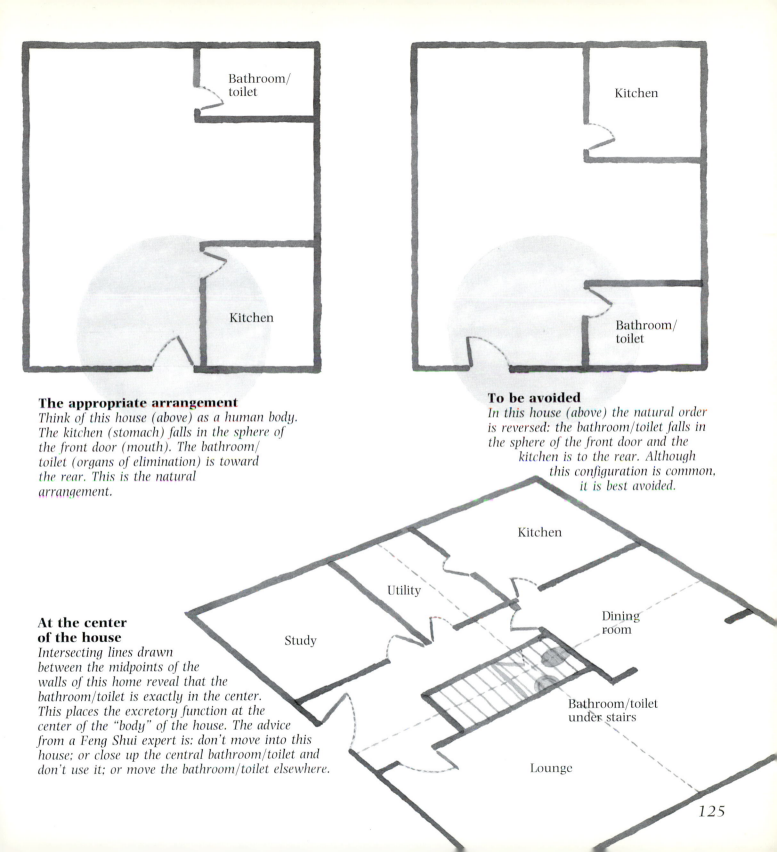

The appropriate arrangement

Think of this house (above) as a human body. The kitchen (stomach) falls in the sphere of the front door (mouth). The bathroom/toilet (organs of elimination) is toward the rear. This is the natural arrangement.

To be avoided

In this house (above) the natural order is reversed: the bathroom/toilet falls in the sphere of the front door and the kitchen is to the rear. Although this configuration is common, it is best avoided.

At the center of the house

Intersecting lines drawn between the midpoints of the walls of this home reveal that the bathroom/toilet is exactly in the center. This places the excretory function at the center of the "body" of the house. The advice from a Feng Shui expert is: don't move into this house; or close up the central bathroom/toilet and don't use it; or move the bathroom/toilet elsewhere.

Bathroom design

The family that fitted out this bathroom consulted a
Feng Shui practitioner before ordering the plumbing
and the fittings. The position of the door in relation
to the toilet, and the way in which the door opens
has been carefully designed, so that anyone using
the toilet has an additional sense of privacy. The
same applies to anyone sitting in the bath tub. The
relative location of the bath tub and toilet has been
worked out so that, although they are in the same
room, they are not immediately next to each other.
The position of the hand basin takes into account
the presence of the mirror: it is not facing the doorway or the window and therefore the tendency for
mirrors to bounce energy backward and forward
and disturb the environment is minimized.

The use of a roller blind on the bathroom
window adjusts the flow of energy in the room and
note that the window is not directly opposite the
door, nor does it overlook or open behind the basin,
toilet, or bath tub.

Unfortunately, whether you are renting or buying a home or are designing a new one, you will
find that very little attention is paid to a good layout for the bathroom. It is either thought of as a
mere utility room, or else efforts are made to dress
it up almost as if to disguise its purpose. In the
human body it would be as if the eliminative needs
of the body were completely ignored. A recent
development has been the incorporation of the
bathroom into the bedroom area, as en suite
facilities, which are now increasingly being
installed in homes.

Separate functions

En suite bathrooms are normally the rule in modern hotels, as the floor plan for this one shows (above). That's fine for commercial travellers and tourists, who will spend only a few days in that sort of environment. But in your own home the rules of Feng Shui strongly advise a clear separation of the functions and energies of the bedroom and the bathroom. If you do have an en suite bathroom, keep the door closed at all times.

127

Plotting your garden

If you have a garden, it is a significant element of your living environment and deserves to be treated with the proper respect. It is not just an extension of your house: it is a space in its own right. If you are thinking about how to design your garden or choosing a home with a garden, you can apply The Five Animals (see pp. 38-9) as illustrated on these pages. The tortoise side of your garden, whether it is a front or back garden, is determined by the wall of your house. The phoenix aspect of the garden is the end of the plot farthest away from the home. Thus, in the main picture on these pages, the back wall of the house faces the larger part of the garden at the rear. So that wall is the tortoise side of both the house and the garden.

The power of trees
Trees are extremely powerful fields of energy, some of nature's most powerful transformers. They have had a special place in the Chinese cultural tradition for centuries. The positioning of trees is therefore of great importance. As a general principle, they should not be too close to your house, but are best placed on the dragon side and toward the phoenix aspect (the far end).

Different levels
Some gardens are built on a slope. And if you are planning a garden, you may want to landscape a slope in it. There are three appropriate arrangements. A level garden, with no slope, is always suitable. Or you can slightly raise the level of the garden behind your house, giving strength to the tortoise side of your home. If you wish to have a contour in the garden itself, the highest point should be on the dragon side of the plot (the left side as you look into the garden from your home).

Water in your garden
The positioning of water around your house is of great importance in Feng Shui, following the principles of the I Ching (see pp. 24-5 and 76-7). The inset plot (above) shows how to determine where to place ponds or other bodies of water: they should always be in the front two quadrants and never to the rear.

Shrub energy

Low-level shrubs and flower beds are best placed on the tiger side of your garden (on the right-hand side as you face the garden from your home). Their low-lying, intense energy is most appropriate in this position. Try to keep the far end of the garden somewhat clear – so that the phoenix aspect is not entirely blocked.

Up, down, in front, and behind

In one sense your home has clearly defined boundaries. You rent or own a property that is legally determined and usually marked out by walls between dwellings, or fences between plots of land. Much of the art of Feng Shui is concerned with harmonious arrangements within those boundaries. But the art also goes beyond those limits because, as explained in Part One, your home is part of many, far larger, configurations of energy. So you would be well advised to pay careful attention to the energetic influences that surround your home in all directions.

If you are looking at properties, find out what's underneath, above, in front, and behind them. Property deeds or local authority records will indicate the previous use of the land before the present building was built. Try to find somewhere that has had a history of good land use. Then look skyward. Living under the flight path of airplanes is definitely not recommended – as anyone who lives under one knows (even though the conscious mind has a way of blocking out that awareness over time). See if you are in the pathway or shadow of tall buildings in front or to the sides or under electricity supply lines: avoid such locations. Is there any space in front of you or are you jammed into a narrow street? And out the back – are there commuter rail lines, city train lines, canals, or highway fly-overs? All these create perpetual disturbance, not only to the physical fabric of homes, but to the health and wellbeing of all who live close to them.

Garden shapes

Gardens come in all shapes and sizes. When deciding how to arrange your garden or where to place it, remember the fundamental principles of The Five Energies theory in Part One (see pp. 32-3) and the information on shapes in Part Two (see pp. 86-7). As with the internal design of your home, Feng Shui is not concerned solely with how attractive your surroundings are but with the effect that they have upon you. It is important to remember that shapes are not neutral entities – they have a power of their own, so even if the interior of your home is arranged according to Feng Shui principles, if your garden is not, your life will be influenced by the potentially negative effects from the land around you.

A well-defined area
Don't try to squeeze your garden into all available crannies. Let it be a well-defined area, such as this obvious open space at the back of the house (above left). Other areas can be given over to grass, gravel, flagstone, or cement.

Long, narrow shapes
The same principle applies if you live in a long, narrow house or have a narrow rectangular garden (above). Try to make a clear distinction between garden and home. Use any remaining areas near the building for other purposes.

Completing the rectangle
In both homes, there is a L-shaped area to the right rear of the building. This could be converted to a conservatory/greenhouse (see pp. 134-5) or patio to complete the rectangle of the building – clearly defined and separate from the garden.

Protect your garden
As with your home, follow The Five Energies theory and arrange your garden to protect it from incoming energy movements.

The ideal setting
In this shape, the ideal position for the garden, in relation to the house, is the area just behind the house and slightly to the dragon-side of the building.

Triangular plot
In this unusually shaped plot (below), it is best to divide the area into distinct segments to create "separate" gardens, or clearly identified sections — a flower garden and a large lawn area with shrubs.

Irregular-shaped plot
In this plot (above), the recommended position for your garden is on the dragon side of the house rather than to the rear (tortoise position), since there is insufficient space behind the house and the effect of a garden there would be to weaken the tortoise aspect of the house itself.

133

Garden energies

Energy flows through and around gardens just as it does in other environments, affecting those in them and near by. Shapes affect that flow (see pp. 86-7 and 132-3). If you construct a conservatory/greenhouse, it changes the shape of your home. The ideal Feng Shui home is a complete rectangle, so if you add a conservatory/greenhouse to one side or to the back, and thereby change the shape of your home into a slightly lopsided figure, you are going against Feng Shui principles. If at all possible, try to construct the conservatory/greenhouse so that it extends fully along one side of a complete rectangle (**3**, right). Or, if your house is already shaped like an L or a U (**1** and **2**, right), then you can construct the conservatory/ greenhouse to fill those vacant spaces and complete the rectangle of your dwelling.

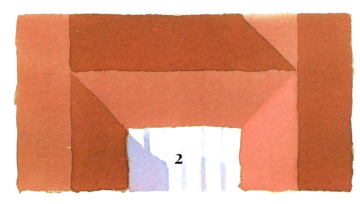

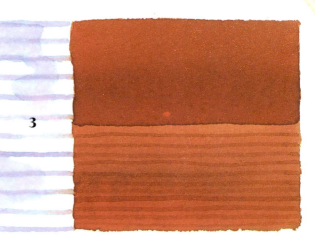

A straight flow-through

The energy flow can pass through your home and garden just as it does inside houses (pp. 48-9). Unfortunately, this common arrangement allows a straight flow-through from the very front of the property to the very back end of the rear garden. There is the added problem of the swimming pool at the back of the house. This is a good example of a situation where professional Feng Shui advice would be needed – to advise on the repositioning of the front door or other steps that could be taken to minimize potential negative effects.

A Feng Shui garden
To plan your Feng Shui garden, keep the central area clear. The tallest bushes should flourish on the dragon side; low shrubs and flowers on the tiger side. Trees should be some distance from the house, but ensure some sense of light and openness for the phoenix aspect.

Pathways

The same principles that govern entrances and exits in your home apply to your garden. Straight avenues are like arrows speeding toward their target. Pathways in your garden should be kept to the sides. Any path leading to your home is best laid out in a gentle curve.

Where you work

The location of your shop, office, or factory is just as important to its success – and to the wellbeing of the people who work there – as the location of your home is to you and your family.

Some of the same principles apply. For example, the patterns of the flow of energy can affect a commercial location just as they do a domestic setting. So you would be unwise to choose a site where your business was likely to be exposed to potentially harmful energy or to road accidents and floods!

There are different considerations when it comes to shops, offices, and factories. The whole point of opening a shop is that you want people to come in to buy your products or services. So it follows naturally that it should be located where there is easy access and, preferably, where there are a lot of passersby. Typically, you will find banks, clothing stores, and all sorts of other such establishments on the corners of busy intersections and grouped together in particular areas to attract as many potential customers as possible. In that way, the guiding principle is different to the tranquillity you would seek when looking for a private residence.

The location of an office, on the other hand, should be determined by relatively easy access. But it should not be exposed to the same level of hustle and bustle that you would expect outside the entrance of a shop. In other words, offices should be in a "quiet corner" of a busy area. Often, this means a side street adjacent to a major intersection or on the upper floors of a building above the shops at street level.

Most factories need space, room to expand and, usually, some open ground for off-site storage and transport requirements. They are noisy places and many produce fumes and waste. Not surprisingly, most zoning regulations separate factories from residential areas. They should have space of their own, where they have a minimal impact on others.

Disturbed energy
The energy at this downtown intersection will be very disturbed, particularly if the streets have two-way traffic. There will also be a lot of pedestrian traffic. Most of us are exposed to short periods of disturbed energy every day. That is not a problem, as long as we are moving around ourselves or just dropping in. This location would be most unsuitable for a house, for example, but would be ideal for a shop that aims to attract casual passersby: a clothes store, a sports shop, an outlet for theatre tickets, a bank, or a travel agent.

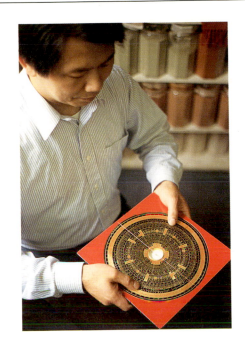

Even to this day, in determining locations of modern businesses or assessing the appropriate arrangement of furniture in the home, Feng Shui masters use the traditional implement of their art – the Lo Pan. This is the specialized compass of Feng Shui, fashioned by experts and meant to be used only by those authorized to do so. The design of the Lo Pan varies, but all have certain common features – visible in this compass held by Master Lam. There is a small metal needle at the center, used to locate the Magnetic North Pole. Two intersecting threads cross the entire board of the Lo Pan and by turning the outer rings of the board these threads can be used as coordinates to bring the board into alignment with the central compass. Radiating out from the center are numerous concentric rings containing essential information on conjunctions of energy, planetary movements, magnetic correlations, and the Chinese calendar.

Too high, not mighty

Supposing you are looking for a new office and a leasing agent tells you there is a superb property with a magnificent view on the thirtieth floor of a new office block. To attract new tenants, the first year's rent is being kept deliberately low. What do you decide to do? You ought to consider the overall site as well as the facilities and suitability of the interior of the new office. You should look carefully at the height of the surrounding buildings. Bear in mind the template of The Five Animals (see pp. 38-9). These drawings offer a simplified guide.

You may feel spontaneously attracted to this office because it overlooks everyone else. It has an unobstructed view and it seems to express something you like about the strength, vision, and power of the corporation that occupies it. But ponder the wisdom of occupying this location very carefully. In the Chinese classic, *The Art of War*, now available in several popular translations in the West, the master, Sun Tze warns: "military formation is like water – the form of water is to avoid staying in high places..." So, even if you have great financial ambition, the best place to achieve it may not be from a lofty, exposed office.

Office 1
This arrangement of buildings conforms to The Five Animals template. The building in front has adequate support to the rear, a dragon and tiger on either side, and a suitable open space in front. It may not be as high and imposing a building as the corner tower, but your Feng Shui knowledge up to this point tells you that this is a far preferable location.

2

Office 2

Up on the 30th floor there is no obstruction in any direction. You can see over the entire city – and everyone can see you. Think back to the house on the hill (see pp. 72-3). In this office, you will be just like a nail on top a piece of wood, waiting to be knocked down.

Inside the office block

A long corridor

This is a common arrangement for the floor of an office tower (left). The corridor may be much longer and there may be other features, but there are common Feng Shui problems in this arrangement. The energy that enters through the doorway will simply pass out through the window. If there is a mirror at the end of the hall, the energy will rebound in disturbed patterns in the hallway. It is best to place a curtain over the window of corridors like this. The room doors are directly opposite each other, setting up potential energy conflicts. In this arrangement, try to keep your door closed.

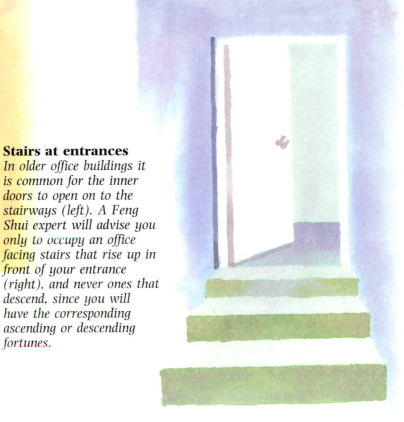

Stairs at entrances

In older office buildings it is common for the inner doors to open on to the stairways (left). A Feng Shui expert will advise you only to occupy an office facing stairs that rise up in front of your entrance (right), and never ones that descend, since you will have the corresponding ascending or descending fortunes.

No front door

Sometimes large corporations take a whole floor or more of an office tower and the elevator opens straight on to the office (left). This is like having no front door. From the point of view of the energy in the office, there should be a definite barrier between the elevator and the main space of the office, since every time the elevator doors open the effect is like a puncture in a tire – the whole airspace is disturbed.

Desks and doors

Many people work in offices where there are several desks, either in rows or facing each other. This almost invariably means that some of the positions are more favourable than others.

In line with the door
The two desks in line with the door (right) could hardly be in a worse position. A Feng Shui practitioner would warn you that the people sitting in those positions are not likely to stay in their jobs for long. More likely than not, they will leave your employment – although they may not be consciously aware that the reason is related to the poor location of their work areas.

A favorable far corner
The only two people in this room (left) with favorable work spaces are the two at the far corner opposite the door. The two in line with the door will have the same problem as in the preceding arrangement, and the person with a desk along the wall beside the door will always have a sense of insecurity, since it is not possible to see the door from the desk.

Back to the window

In the office (left), regardless of whether other people share it or not, the person who has a desk with their back to the window is violating the basic instructions of The Five Animal template (see pp. 38-9). If, instead of a window, they are sitting with their back to a mirror, they will be constantly subjected to reverberating energy.

Perpetual target

Here (above) the door opens directly opposite the desk at the far end of the room and the person acts as a perpetual target for energy slicing through the room. The desks on either side of the room are spared that, and all have the support of a wall at their backs.

145

Out in the open

Some offices still consist of an army of desks, lined up in formation on a wide open parade square, with everyone forced to work under the constant pressure of overhead strip lighting. This is not an office that is likely to promote the health of its employees, create an environment for clear thinking, or win genuine respect for the management.

If you are given a desk in the middle of the floor, your back will be on an open "corridor" along which people are passing. Your back will be vulnerable to bumps and your nervous system will always be on the alert. With desks in front and on either side, chances are that both your creativity and your concentration will suffer.

If this is your only chance for a job, you may have to accept it. But for your own sake, don't plan on staying there for long!

If possible, don't work in an office that has a bathroom/toilet opening directly on to the main work area, either. This arrangement stems from office managers wanting to keep an eye on staff spending long periods in the bathroom/toilet. This kind of attitude is still around: it is bad for staff morale and a very poor arrangement from the Feng Shui point of view.

Water is always a problem in the world of Feng Shui. It is better to have a completely separate area for anything involving water since it can have such a potent effect on the surroundings. If you want to have a sink in your work area or a place for making tea and coffee, the best advice is to consult a Feng Shui expert before installing the facilities.

A photocopier sets up a considerable disturbance in the energy field and, particularly if it is a large one and in use a great deal of the time, should be put in a room of its own or in an area separate from normal offices and desks.

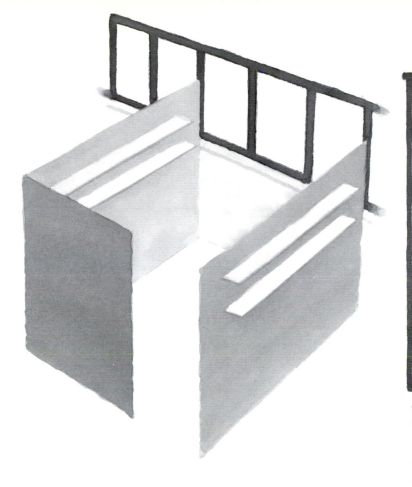

ROOM PLAN

Desk

Visitor's chair

Computer table

Chair

Filing cabinet

Applying Feng Shui to an office workstation
The problem of the open-plan office has been recognized to some extent, and people are being offered workstations with some privacy. Supposing you are lucky enough to get a space beside the window. Your space is marked out with partitions. You have to fit in a desk and desk chair, a visitor's chair, a filing cabinet, and a computer stand. Think of the partitions as walls and the entry space as the door (except you could change the door position) – assume the flow of energy will be basically the same as in a normal room. Use The Five Animals template (see pp. 38-9) and the information on pages 144-7 to determine the best location for the various items.

The open-plan landscape

Many open-plan office schemes are available these days with sophisticated workstation arrangements, including built-in communications and computer facilities. They look a lot better than the old-fashioned office on pages 146-7. But looks aren't everything. What may seem very attractive to a prospective client and efficient from the point of view of technical configurations, may not look quite the same to a Feng Shui expert. Let's examine what's happening in this open-plan office.

Direct entry
*The door (**1**) opens directly on to the office area. As with the elevator on pages 140-1, the energy of the whole office will be disturbed in some way every time someone enters*

No backing
*Most of the desks (**2**) are arranged so that people face a partition, exposing their backs. This has the subliminal effect of making people feel that they are on their own. They end up feeling nervous. From a manager's point of view, this seating arrangement has the negative effect of making staff feel that they are "not being given any backing".*

Cutting edge
*Partitions (**3**) positioned like this act as sharp lines cutting up the energy of the internal space. Their strong energies slice across the space from one desk to another, like meat cleavers targetted on nearby and distant desks. Their effect is to create competition, jealousy, and arguments.*

Turned outward

*This person (**4**) has turned the desk to face away from the wall. This is a good adjustment, although in the overall conditions, its effect will be limited. At least there is support on the back and some space toward the front.*

4

6

Central conflict

*In the center are the office files (**5**) and the photo-copier. The photocopier is Yang and the files are Yin. In this case they are in conflict and neither belongs in the center of a room: the photocopier creates distur-bance and the files have a deadening quality.*

Screened off

*Most people sit facing computers (**6**) for long periods. Usually they are far too close to the screen for their own health. This is an office in which virtu-ally everyone's "phoenix aspect" is blocked. The result is a distinct lack of imagination and creativity (see pp. 38-9 for the quali-ties associated with the phoenix).*

In a tiny office

You get a tiny office of your own. There is a door and a window and on one wall there is shelving. You need to arrange your desk and desk chair, a visitor's chair, and a filing cabinet. That's all you have room for. You can only think of five realistic options, but which one is best?

More vulnerable
The energy pathway (above) is the same, but now you have put your back to the door. You can see out of the window, so it is less claustrophobic, but your back is even more exposed and vulnerable and the back of your neck and head are directly in the current between the door and the window.

Exposed position
The energy pathway from the door (above) to the window will pass directly across your chair. The effect will be to make you feel uncomfortable if you spend long periods in that position, probably without realizing why. This will be made all the worse by the fact that your back is exposed and you cannot see who is entering the room. You will feel even more constricted by facing the wall.

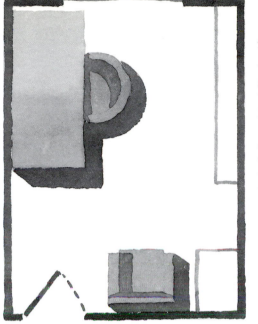

An improvement

You have a better sense of who is coming into the room, which is also more welcoming to visitors. But you are still cut off by the wall in front of your desk, your back is unsupported, and you are sitting in the current between the door and the window.

Out of the current

In this arrangement (left), you have moved out of the way of the current between the door and the window and you have a clear line of sight to the door. Your back is relatively supported, although part of it is exposed to the window. You should draw the blinds across that part of the window. The position of your visitors is not satisfactory, but this is a temporary location for them.

Better backing

The visitor's position is still a problem, but in this arrangement (above), your back is in a good position, you have space in front, can see the door and you sit out of the energy current. Make sure the wall shelves do not extend over your head.

Computer inputs

One object that you have to take into account today, which certainly did not feature in the ancient evolution of Feng Shui, is the computer.

A badly designed reception area

You work as a receptionist. Your employer decides that in addition to answering the telephone and receiving guests you should do data entry on a computer. Instead of redesigning your work area (right), the office manager finds a way of placing a computer in your existing space by cramming it into a wall niche You are forced to turn your back to the door and sit far too close to the screen. It is a prescription for claustrophobia. You can also see how poor the rest of the design is: there is a counter which cuts off the space in front of you and the area for guests is adjacent to the door – not the best way to put them at their ease.

152

A "luxury" workstation

This commercial workstation (right) advertises itself as a luxury, fashioned in polished wood. But it is like a coffin and from the Feng Shui point of view might just as well be one. It has a recessed low VDU screen, causing your head to tilt forward, placing unhealthy pressure on the back of your neck.

Modular arrangement

This three-sided modular desk (left) gives you much greater flexibility in adapting your work area to your office or home. If the main forward direction is in the direction of the arrow, you would be advised to put the modular section with the computer screen on your dragon side.

Working at home

What happens if you are one of the increasing number of people who undertake freelance work at home? If you have the space, you may be able to convert one of your rooms into a small office, in which case you can adapt the information in this part of the book to meet your circumstances.

But supposing you don't have all that much extra space and you need to accommodate some work space in another room, say a spare bedroom? You will find yourself having to make choices and compromises. The part of the room which has the bed will be for a Yin purpose and the area where you set up your office will for a Yang purpose – each has different requirements. In order to determine how best to arrange the room you need to determine the main use of the room: is it primarily a bedroom that is used from time to time for office work, or is it the other way around? Taking the primary use into account is the best rule of thumb for deciding some of the basic questions.

For example, here are the floor plans of a small bedroom, arranged according to two primary uses. In Plan 1, the bed is in the best possible location in relation to door and window, but there are drawbacks in the way the desk has been arranged. This would be appropriate if the main use of the room was as a bedroom. If the main use was as an office (Plan 2), you could switch the bed and desk so that the bed was on the same side as the door (less suitable) and position the desk more toward the center of the room, allowing you space to sit behind it with your back to the wall. The screen helps protect the sleeping space.

In all such considerations, don't burden yourself with trying to come up with the absolutely perfect solution. There is no such concept in Feng Shui. You must take as many aspects into account as possible, try to decide which are the most important, and see what you can do to accommodate them harmoniously.

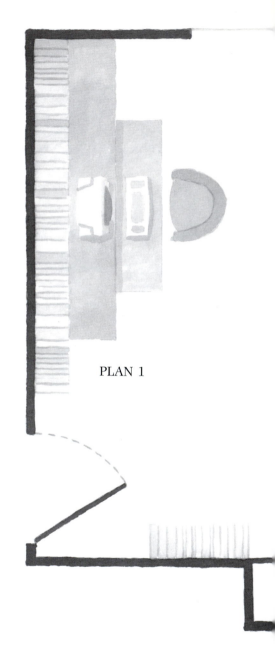

PLAN 1

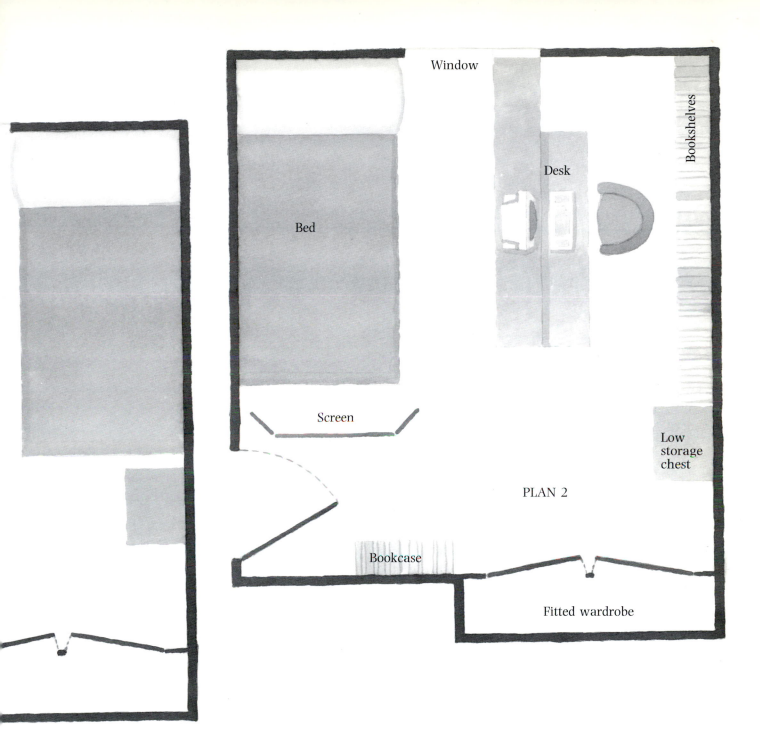

Window

Bed

Bookshelves

Desk

Screen

Low
storage
chest

PLAN 2

Bookcase

Fitted wardrobe

AUTHOR'S ACKNOWLEDGMENTS

It is a rare opportunity to be able to enter the world of Feng Shui, this mysterious and ancient art. This would never have been possible for me, but for the four masters who accepted me as their student. When I was very young in Hong Kong I was first introduced in my teens to the arts of Chinese culture by Master Lau Sau Hong. My next teacher in Hong Kong was Master Lee Chuen Lun under whom I studied throughout the 1970s. After that I was fortunate to be able to learn from Master Wang Chung Han in Taiwan. Most recently Master Ho Chiu Hong in Hong Kong kindly agreed to help me with my studies. To these remarkable human beings I offer my deep gratitude.

I also want to say how much I owe to my wife, Kai Sin, and my three sons, Tin Yun, Tin Yu and Tin Hun. They have stood by me when it has sometimes been very difficult to make a living in the West and to gain acceptance in this culture for the ideas and traditions of the Chinese Way.

This book would not have been published but for the willingness of Gaia Books to undertake this challenge. I want to express my gratitude to the Managing Director, Joss Pearson, for deciding to make this commitment. The project was then pursued with enthusiasm and insight by the Managing Editor, Pip Morgan, and the Art Director, Patrick Nugent, who spent many hours developing the framework and design for this book.

This was always going to be a difficult undertaking and I needed the support of a brilliant designer and a first class editor. Bridget Morley devoted herself with great intelligence and sensitivity to the design, meticulously directed the artist, Sally Launders, and supervised the photo selection. My student, Richard Reoch, worked closely with us to help translate the elusive concepts of the Feng Shui universe into a text that I believe will help readers in all parts of the world cross a new threshold of understanding.

Finally, I would like to thank the rest of those at Gaia Books who guided this book through its final stages.

Feng Shui consultations and advice: *Anyone wishing an individual consultation for their home or business from Master Lam may contact him at his clinic: First Floor, 70 Shaftesbury Avenue, London W1V 7DF, United Kingdom. Telephone: (44) 171 287 2114 or (44) 0831 802 598. Fax: (44) 171 437 3118. Master Lam is often invited to travel in Europe and the United States for consultations and lectures. For personalized, basic information about your own attributes according to the Five Energies system and the Chinese Calendar, and the relevant colors and directions that you can use in your home or at work, please send a self-addressed envelope to the Lam Clinic requesting further details and fees.*

ABOUT THE AUTHOR

Master Lam Kam Chuen is a fully qualified practitioner of Feng Shui who has been training in this art for most of his life. He has studied under four masters in Hong Kong and Taiwan, each of whom is an acknowledged master in specialized aspects of Feng Shui.

Now that there is a growing interest in Feng Shui outside the Chinese world, Master Lam was persuaded to create a Feng Shui handbook, partly because he was concerned to preserve the tradition in its correct form.

Master Lam is also a recognized master of the arts of Tai Chi and Chi Kung, and a practitioner of Traditional Chinese Medicine. He was born in Hong Kong shortly after the Second World War and at a very early age began his training in traditional Chinese arts.

As a young man he became a qualified bonesetter and herbalist, and opened a school and clinic in Hong Kong. He also undertook the painstaking study of Chi Kung, a system for the cultivation of internal energy in the body. Using his medical skills and his knowledge of Chi Kung he began to develop a new form of Tai Chi, now known as Lam Style Tai Chi.

Master Lam came to the West in 1976 when he became the first Tai Chi instructor appointed to teach in the Inner London Education Authority. In 1987, he gave the first European demonstration of the art of Zhan Zhuang Chi Kung, which he studied in Beijing under Professor Yu Yong Nian, the world's leading authority. He now teaches and practices medicine at The Lam Clinic in London's Chinatown.

Following the widely acclaimed BBC series, *The Way of the Warrior*, Master Lam was invited to act as consultant to the sequel publication, *The Way of Harmony*. This was followed by his ground-breaking work published by Gaia Books, *The Way of Energy*, introducing the Zhan Zhuang Chi Kung system of Standing Like a Tree, and *Step-by-Step Tai Chi*.

Master Lam has become familiar to television viewers as a result of the 1995 TV series, *Stand Still – Be Fit*, which is also now available under the same title on video. New videos on Tai Chi and Chi Kung will be released in the future.

INDEX

THE COMPLETE WOMAN'S HERBAL

A Manual of Healing Herbs and Nutrition
for Personal Well-Being and Family Care
by Anne McIntyre

Women who want a healthy diet and lifestyle coupled with the use of medicinal herbs can now turn to *The Complete Woman's Herbal*.

This thoroughly researched work by a director of the National Institute of Medical Herbalists is divided into three main sections and fully illustrated in color throughout. The first section is an overview of herbal well-being; the second deals with the various stages of a woman's life; and the third offers practical problem-solving advice, all focusing on the use of herbs and nutrition for physical and emotional health.

With appendices that include a glossary of terms, a directory of organizations, including herb suppliers, and further reading, *The Complete Woman's Herbal* is a compendium of healthy alternatives and an indispensable guide for all health-conscious women.

0-8050-3537-0 • $25.00 • pb •
288 pp. • hundreds of full-color illustrations
Available at all bookstores

A HENRY HOLT REFERENCE BOOK
HENRY HOLT AND COMPANY, INC.
115 WEST 18TH STREET
NEW YORK, NY 10011

The Complete
WOMAN'S
HERBAL

A manual of healing herbs
and nutrition for personal
wellbeing and family care

ANNE McINTYRE